D1372700

ONE BODY AND ONE SPIRIT

A STUDY OF THE CHURCH IN THE

NEW TESTAMENT

BY OSCAR J. F. SEITZ

GREENWICH · CONNECTICUT · 1960

© 1960 by The Seabury Press, Incorporated

Library of Congress Catalog Card Number: 60-11084

Design by Stefan Salter

Printed in the United States of America

All scriptural quotations in this book, unless otherwise indicated, are taken from *The Holy Bible, Revised Standard Version,* copyrights 1946, 1952, by the Division of Christian Education of the National Council of Churches of Christ in the United States of America.

In conformity to biblical usage capitals have not been used in pronouns referring to God, nor in references to the church, in whatever sense the term is used.

329-760-C-3.5

to R U T H

a constant companion in all these studies

2017

CONTENTS

For just as the body is one and has many members, and all the members of the body, though many, are one body, so it is with Christ. For by one Spirit we were all baptized into one body—Jews or Greeks, slaves or free—and all were made to drink of one Spirit.

I Corinthians 12:12-13

INTRODUCTION

THE FIRST records of the Christian church are contained in the New Testament. It is important to remember that the earliest, as well as the most enduring, result of the life and teaching of Jesus was not a book. It was a community of people whose purpose it was to be led by his spirit. Jesus himself wrote nothing that was ever preserved. He entrusted his message and mission to a company of disciples who were already members of a "church," the ancient congregation of Israel. That congregation traced its origin to a covenant which God had made with its forefathers. The law of Moses was its charter. Within that Jewish church the disciples appeared as a small sect holding one distinctive belief. It was their faith that Jesus is the Messiah, or Christ, that eventually earned for them the name of Christians. The charter of their common life was the gospel.

In a memorable contrast between the law and the gospel, Paul expressed the confidence that through Christ the living God has established a new covenant with his people, "not in a written code, but in the Spirit." (II Corinthians 3:4-18) For reasons which will be examined in our study, the English translation of 1611 used the word "testament," instead of "covenant," in this passage. Consequently, it has become customary to refer to the scriptures in which the two covenants are recorded as the books of the Old and New Testaments.

For a Christian reader today, the Bible without the New Testament is unthinkable. He can hardly imagine a time in the history

1

2017

of his faith when these twenty-seven books were not known and read by the followers of Christ. Yet the Christian faith was nearly twenty years old before the earliest of these books was written, and another century passed before the last book was finished. Even then, and for some years following, not all Christian communities everywhere possessed or acknowledged all of these books. It was not until the fourth century that the New Testament, as a collection of holy scriptures generally recognized as equal in authority to the Old Testament, was brought to final completion. Yet during that long period, the Christian fellowship had grown from a tiny persecuted sect to a community of world-wide influence, proclaiming the gospel of Jesus Christ to all mankind.

The books of the Holy Bible are our primary source of information regarding the nature of the church in its beginnings. Few pages of the New Testament do not presuppose some knowledge of the Old. The very idea of belonging to a church at all is an important part of the biblical inheritance of Christianity from Judaism. Consequently, the opening chapters of such a study as this must take the reader back into the sacred scriptures of the Jewish church: the law and the prophets and the other writings. For although the community of believers in Christ can rightly be called a "new creation," the church can show a real continuity with its historic past. This continuity is maintained in the New Testament, where Christians are occasionally referred to by such symbolic terms as "the Israel of God," or "the twelve tribes in the dispersion." (Galatians 6:16; James 1:1)

Outside the collections of books which now make up the Holy Bible, there are other early Christian writings of great antiquity, some of them as old as the latest books of the New Testament itself. Important among these are a group known as *The Apostolic Fathers.* The chief significance of this title is that these writings were believed to preserve traditions which went back to the time of the apostles. In our study we shall find it useful to examine some of these traditions, evaluating them in the light of the holy scriptures.

Current interest in the discovery of a collection of Hebrew documents hidden in a cave in the wilderness of Judea has prompted the author to add to his original manuscript occasional references to the so-called "Dead Sea Scrolls." On a recent visit to Palestine, he had opportunity not only to see the Scrolls and the area in which they were found, but to talk with some of the archeologists, paleographers, philologists, and other scholars doing original research in this field. Some of the more popular books about the Scrolls have advanced conflicting and sometimes extravagant claims regarding the relation of their contents to early Christianity. Already some of the more sensational opinions have been corrected, sometimes by the work of critics, sometimes by the writers themselves. The general position taken in this book is on the more conservative side, since the author is convinced that it will take many years of careful study before the more controversial issues can be cleared up. The value of these documents for students of the New Testament can be determined only through reference to specific passages, some of which we shall have occasion to observe as we proceed.

In the course of this book the author has had to deal with a number of other matters on which serious differences of opinion exist among biblical scholars and theologians, as well as among Christians in general. Many of his own opinions have undergone modification during the years of study which the writing of even these short chapters has required. He has attempted to face these issues honestly and humbly, frequently indicating areas in which both agreement and disagreement are to be found. It is his hope that in this way each reader may be stimulated to further thought and study, including discussion with others. In his conclusion, he has ventured to offer some suggestions regarding the value of group study of the Bible, which he trusts may help to carry the reader forward after he has closed the book.

A study of the church in the New Testament is of vital concern to every Christian who wishes to understand the nature of his faith and of the fellowship to which he belongs. Such an understanding is especially needed today, when Christian people are seeking to reaffirm their unity in Christ. All Christians—whatever be their denomination—read the same Bible, although in different versions and tongues. All appeal to the New Testament as the ultimate source of their varying traditions. All alike, though holding somewhat different views about the authority of the scriptures, believe that the doctrines and practices of their particular communion are based upon the word of God.

The New Testament stands as a constant reminder to Christians that, because there is one God and Father of us all, one Lord, one Spirit, we are called to be "one body." The essential unity of believers in Christ is at once a fact and a goal yet to be realized. Meanwhile, the Spirit of God continues his work in a broken order of our making. As the primary source of our common faith, the New Testament must be the starting point and ultimate meeting point of the great movements toward fuller realization of Christian unity, which are a clear manifestation of the work of the Holy Spirit in our day.

Out of this conviction the writer has undertaken this book, humbly conscious of its limitations and of its need for supplementation from other works, to many of which he is himself indebted. In the appended bibliography, however, he has not attempted to list every publication which he has consulted because many of these are too technical to be of help to the general reader. Instead, he has selected a few of the more representative recent books on the subject which do not require special knowledge of Greek or Hebrew.

Besides books dealing specifically with the early church and its ministry, it has seemed useful to mention here two important conference reports: that of the First Assembly of the World Council of Churches, at Amsterdam, 1948, which includes several representative interpretations of the doctrine of the church as held in various communions; and that of the Lambeth Conference of Bishops of the Anglican Communion, assembled in 1958, which contains resolutions and reports concerning the authority and message of the Holy Bible, and Church Unity.

In one of their resolutions the Bishops at Lambeth declared:

> The Conference welcomes every sign of the revival of Bible Study within the common life of the Church. It calls on all Church people to re-establish the habit of Bible-reading at home, and commends the growing practice of group Bible study. (page 33)

The report of the Committee on Church Unity and the Church Universal closes with the following recommendation:

> It has often been observed that one of the most serious weaknesses of the ecumenical movement is that it draws the divided Churches together 'at the top,' but fails to draw them together equally at the local level, where actual congregations of Christ's flock live and worship side by side. The Committee believes it to be the duty of every bishop to take the lead in promoting this work in his own diocese. It calls upon all our clergy and people to break out of the isolation and introversion of much of our Church life, and to seek, by every means at national and local level, to establish brotherly relationships and contacts and to share perplexities and burdens, that we may be one with our Christian brethren of other traditions in Christ's mission to the world. (page 60)

It is the earnest hope of the author that this book may become instrumental in furthering to some degree the spirit of this resolution and this recommendation.

CHAPTER ONE

JESUS AND THE CONGREGATION OF ISRAEL

In a Jewish synagogue of Galilee, Jesus began his public teaching and with it the prophetic movement which eventually created the Christian church. Within a generation his message had spread across the Roman Empire, and a congregation of his followers was established in its capital city. Not until then did any one attempt to record in writing the story of his life and work. The book which first told the story was the Gospel according to Mark, written about A.D. 65-70, perhaps at Rome.

Mark described the initial event in the ministry of Jesus, which was to have such far reaching consequences, in bare outline:

> And they went into Capernaum; and immediately on the sabbath he entered the synagogue and taught. And they were astonished at his teaching, for he taught them as one who had authority, and not as the scribes. (Mark 1:21-22)

Historical imagination permits us to visualize the scene. Jesus is accompanied by four disciples newly chosen among the fishermen of that neighborhood. Together they pass between stately white columns which frame the entrance to an impressive stone building overlooking the lake of Galilee. Then they disappear from view. Those who wish to follow them further must take the gospel as their first and most reliable guide.

If you visit Palestine, with the text of the New Testament in your hand, you may relive such scenes for yourself. Like the four fishermen-disciples, you can still walk along the northwestern shore of the blue lake, its waters sparkling in the intense brilliance of semi-tropical sunlight. As you approach Tell Hum, the probable site of ancient Capernaum, and pass beneath the welcome shade of a long grove of trees, you may mount the stone steps of a Jewish house of worship unearthed there by modern archeologists. Portions of the fallen masonry have been restored. In front of the north wall stands a row of columns, with capitols in modified Corinthian style, supporting a massive stone lintel. But most of the ornamentation which once adorned this edifice—carved grape vines with wine jars, the star of David, and other familiar symbols—lie strewn about in confusion. You will ask at once, is this the very synagogue building in which Jesus began to teach, the one erected by a Roman centurion friendly to the religion of the Jews? (Luke 7:1-5)

Unfortunately the archeologist must answer No. All that can be seen above ground at this site was probably constructed after the two wars of rebellion against Roman rule, A.D. 66-70 and 132-5, when most Jewish places of assembly were destroyed. Whatever remained of the earlier synagogue at Capernaum may, perhaps, lie beneath the present ruins as part of their foundation, whence it is unlikely it will ever be recovered. It is wise to turn any disappointment we may feel here to good use, for if we should stop to center our attention on the physical features of any building, however ancient, we might easily overlook all that was most vital to the synagogue. To follow those first followers of Jesus beyond the stone façade, and discover more fully the purpose for which they joined their fellow-townsmen that sabbath morning, we need to consider carefully Mark's brief report, supplementing it with others preserved elsewhere in the records of the New Testament.

It is sometimes suggested that the gospel writers were not very well-informed about the synagogues of Palestine, because they gave no description of their furnishings. For example, certain Jewish documents, though of considerably later date than the gospel records, mention such features as the ark, a chest containing the leather scrolls of the *Torah*, or "law" as these scriptures are called in the English Bible. They speak also of the lectern, or stand, on which such a scroll was supported during public reading in the service. But the silence of the evangelists about such accessories provides no evidence that they were ignorant of actual synagogue practice, since the reading and exposition of the scriptures is specifically mentioned. (Luke 4:16-21) Rather, the brevity of their accounts suggests that the gospel writers took for granted a good deal of information on the part of their first readers in order to concentrate their attention on details essential to their own purpose. That purpose was to proclaim the message and mission of Jesus against its original background. The most dominant feature of that background was the presence in virtually every town and village of Palestine of a synagogue building and—something of equal importance—a school where Jewish boys learned to read the sacred scriptures which provided the central content for all synagogue services.

Synagogue, Scriptures, and School

Mark composed his record of the gospel in Greek, a language readily understood by all his first readers. He had no need to explain to any of them what he meant by the word *synagogue*, which was originally a Greek term later borrowed by the English language. At first this word referred, not to a building at all, but to an assembly of people gathered together for a specific purpose. The Jews themselves called the place where such an assembly met "house of the congregation." Another name for it may have been "place of prayer." (Acts 16:13) But occasionally the term *synagogue* was also used as a kind of shorthand description for the meetinghouse. (Luke 7:5; Acts 18:7) However, the original meaning of the word can still be seen in phrases like "those who belonged to the synagogue" for members of the congregation, or "letters to the synagogues" for messages addressed to the assemblies. (Acts 6:9; 9:2)

When the Gospel according to Mark was finished, it was read publicly in a Christian church. We are so familiar with the word *church* in English, that few of us ever stop to inquire where it came from or what it means. For it has a long history which is the exact reverse of the history of the word *synagogue* as a description of a house of worship. Once again we have borrowed from the Greeks, just as the Scots borrowed their word *kirk* and the Germans, *kirche*. The Greek term *kyriakos* means "belonging to the Lord." In the entire New Testament this term was used only twice: once in referring to the Lord's supper; and once to the Lord's day. (I Corinthians 11:20; Revelation 1:10) Several centuries passed before it was similarly used to describe a building erected for Christian worship, known as the Lord's house.

The New Testament contains no reference to any such special "church" buildings. On the contrary, it furnishes ample evidence that the earliest Christians held their meetings in private houses. So Paul addressed a letter: "To Philemon . . . and the church in your house," and in other letters mentioned a church which met in the home of some other Christian. (Romans 16:5; I Corinthians 16:19; Colossians 4:15; Philemon 2) "The church in your house" would be a very curious expression if the word *church* itself referred to a building. The explanation is simple. By the time the first English translations of the Bible were made, this word, which began as the designation of a house of worship, had come to be used for the congregation of people who assembled there. So it was used to translate still another Greek term which, like *synagogue,* originally meant an assembly. That Greek term was *ekklesia,* which left its mark on the English language in various references to ecclesiastical subjects.

The most significant thing about the Christian church was never the place of meeting, but the religious purpose for which believers met. The same was true of the Jewish synagogue. The primary purpose for which its members assembled on the sabbath was to listen to the reading of the holy scriptures, known as the law and the prophets. (Acts 13:15) This practice grew out of one of the fundamental convictions of Judaism. Through inspired teachers of the past God had spoken his word and revealed his will to his people, showing them the way of life which they should obediently follow. (Deuteronomy 30:15-19; Jeremiah 21:8) It was such obedience to the revealed will of God that Jesus had in mind when he said he had come to fulfill the law and the prophets. (Matthew 5:17-18)

Besides these scriptures there were others, known simply as the writings, chief among them being the collection of psalms used in services of the temple at Jerusalem. (Luke 24:44) Upon this whole body of scriptures the religious life of Jesus had been nourished from boyhood, and to them he made constant reference in his teaching. Although the influence of a pious home must have been very important in his life, one cannot imagine the family of a Galilean carpenter owning even a single book of the scriptures. The great leather rolls on which the text of the law had been laboriously inscribed by hand were the most treasured possessions of the synagogue. Due to the costliness of producing such manuscript volumes, private ownership of a roll of scripture must have been rather rare. While the New Testament includes the report of a man riding in a chariot and reading the Book of Isaiah, such an object would have been exceedingly bulky and cumbersome to handle under such circumstances. (Acts 8:28) A complete copy of this very book of the Bible, found among the documents known as the "Dead Sea Scrolls," is composed of seventeen separate pieces of leather carefully sewed together to form a roll approximately twenty-four feet in length, and two feet in height. Yet this was not an unusually large book in antiquity. Greek rolls often ran to a length of thirty feet, while much longer scrolls were used among the Egyptians.

Most Jewish boys gained familiarity with the sacred scriptures by going to school, as well as by regular attendance at the weekly meetings of the congregation. One of the evangelists preserved the picture of Jesus at the age of twelve, as an eager and inquiring student "sitting among the teachers, listening to them and asking them questions." (Luke 2:46)

A Jewish elementary school was called "house of the book," and the first book a boy learned to read was one of the five books of the law, Leviticus. The language in which this and nearly every other portion of the Jewish scriptures were written was Hebrew, though a few passages were composed in a sister language, Aramaic. (Ezra 4:7—6:18, 7:12-26; Daniel 2:4—7:28) Long before the time of Jesus, Aramaic had become the spoken language of Palestine, while Hebrew was used principally in the schools and for the scripture readings in the synagogue. Consequently, such readings were always followed by an interpretation in the language which the people spoke and understood. For centuries after Christ none of these Aramaic paraphrases was permitted to be written down so that they might not become a substitute for the Bible itself.

The Hebrew scriptures were the Bible not only of the Jewish synagogue, but also of the Christian church during its first years. Later, Christians came to speak of them as the books of the Old Testament, to distinguish them from the writings known as the books of the New Testament. Since the New Testament cannot be understood without the aid of the Old Testament, these ancient Hebrew books continue to be one of the most valuable treasures that Christianity has inherited from Judaism. However, since the writers of the various books which make up our New Testament not only composed their works in Greek, but frequently quoted the Old Testament scriptures in that language, it is important to observe how a Greek Bible came into circulation before the time of Christ.

The Bible Among the Greeks

Not all Jews at the time of Jesus lived in Palestine. Many of them had become residents of various neighboring or distant lands, first to the east, later to the west. Some had gone as captives of war, while others had emigrated voluntarily. In either case, wherever they settled, even in small numbers, they organized a synagogue since only ten male members were required to constitute such a congregation. In the course of time, however, most of these scattered exiles adopted the language of the people among whom they dwelt. In the lands around the Mediterranean Sea the predominant language for several centuries had been Greek.

The period following the conquests of Alexander the Great, when a single language facilitated communication between the different peoples of that vast region, has been called the Hellenistic Age. Those Jews who adopted that common language, the language of Hellas or Greece, are therefore known as Hellenistic Jews. Occasionally some of these Greek-speaking Jews or their descendents returned to Palestine, and there they established their own assemblies since they had not kept up the use of their mother tongue. There were such Hellenists among the early disciples at Jerusalem, while among their opponents were men belonging to a synagogue of the Freedmen. Evidently these freedmen were liberated Jewish captives who had been repatriated from various parts of the empire, including Alexandria, a city of Egypt founded by Alexander the Great. (Acts 6:1, 9) There was a large Jewish population in that city, and one of the most significant results of Hellenistic Judaism began there. This was the translation of the holy scriptures into Greek. Unlike the Aramaic-speaking Jews of Palestine, the Hellenists showed no scruples against putting such material in written form. Owing to its great importance, the law was translated first, some time during the third century before Christ. The translation of the prophets and other writings followed during the next two centuries. This earliest Greek version of the Bible soon came into general use among Hellenistic Jews in other regions. It is known as the Septuagint, or the version of the seventy elders.

The primary purpose for which this Greek Bible was published was to insure the continued education of Hellenistic Jews in the basic principles of their ancestral faith. But it soon became an effective instrument for the conversion of such Gentiles as might be admitted to the synagogue to hear its message. So Paul was able to address in the same congregation not only "men of Israel," but others described as "God-fearers" or "devout Greeks." (Acts 13:16; 17:2-4) Such Gentile inquirers into the truths of Judaism occasionally appeared in Palestine. There is a report that some Greeks who had come to Jerusalem to worship asked to see Jesus. (John 12:20)

The progress of the gospel and of the Christian church would have been slower and more difficult, had there not been the regular reading of the Septuagint in the Hellenistic synagogues of the Jewish Dispersion. Not only did Christian missionaries find their first hearers in these congregations, but they were spared the arduous task of making their own independent translation of the Hebrew scriptures. Yet the influence of that pioneer effort in Bible translation has been even more permanent. Since all the books of the New Testament were originally composed in Greek, the existence of the Septuagint still sheds light upon their message. Unfortunately this light is often obscured in the better known English versions of the Bible. Consequently it is necessary for the serious student of the New Testament to look behind these familiar versions, in order to discover how the Septuagint can illuminate the meaning and associations of the Greek word usually translated into English as "church." For this Greek word was repeatedly used in the Old Testament where our English versions never employ the word "church." In other words, English readers need to rediscover the church in the Old Testament.

The Church in the Old Testament

The most familiar English translation of the Holy Bible, called the King James version, was published in 1611. The way had been prepared for it by a long line of earlier translations, beginning with the work of John Wyclif near the end of the fourteenth century. The accuracy of Wyclif's version was seriously marred by his ignorance of the original Hebrew and Greek texts. He was therefore compelled to depend entirely on a Latin version made ten centuries earlier, known as the Vulgate. But in 1526 an English translation of the entire New Testament was made directly from the Greek, followed after a few years by translations of several Old Testament books from the Hebrew. These important steps were taken by William Tyndale.

Immediately there was a storm of criticism so violent that not only copies of his New Testament, but Tyndale himself, was condemned to the flames. One of the leaders of the opposition to Tyndale's version was Sir Thomas More, who accused the translator of intentionally misrepresenting the scriptures. The center of More's attack was Tyndale's use of the word *congregation* in place of *church,* wherever the Greek term *ekklesia* occurred. This, More charged, was simply a repetition of the "heresy" of Luther, who had followed a similar course in his German translation of the New Testament published in 1522.

But if there was error, it was on the side of More, rather than on the part of Luther and Tyndale. For the Greek term *ekklesia* in the New Testament always referred to a gathering of people, and in one place to a disorderly gathering of pagan people who attacked Paul at Ephesus. (Acts 19:32 and 41) Here the King James version, like its modern revisions, has the word "assembly." Wyclif actually used the word *church* for this unruly mob! Further on in this story the term *ekklesia* was used for another kind of gathering, when the Jewish spokesman Alexander urged that the matter in dispute should be settled in "the regular assembly." (Acts 19:39) Wyclif called this "the lawful church." But what Alexander meant was the legally constituted meeting of citizens, called out from their homes to transact public business. This had been the original meaning of the term among the Greeks.

If we ask how it happened that the term *ekklesia* was applied to Christian meetings for worship, we must seek light from the Septuagint. For the makers of that earliest version of the Bible frequently used this term to translate a Hebrew word meaning the "congregation" of Israel gathered in solemn assembly to worship the Lord. (I Kings 8:14) Like the Greek term, this Hebrew word carried with it the idea of a company of people called together. Only these people were convinced that their call had come from God himself. Consequently they were also known as the congregation or assembly of God. (Nehemiah 13:1) We must give Wyclif credit for trying to be consistent, for he translated this phrase as "the church of God" in his version of the Old Testament.

The truth is that the word *church* is no more inappropriate for one part of the Bible than for the other. In the Septuagint the term *ekklesia* was used almost as often as it was in the New Testament. But no one would ever guess this from reading either the King James version or its more recent revisions. Where the Septuagint had the term *ekklesia*, the English translators of 1611 used either "congregation" or "assembly," but never *church*. On the other hand, they were under strict orders not to use the word "congregation" in place of *church* in the New Testament. The result is that few readers of the Bible in English have any way of knowing how closely "the church of God" in early Christian writings was related to "the congregation of the Lord" in the Hebrew scriptures.

Synagogue, too, was a Greek term frequently used in the Septuagint. Sometimes, particularly in Leviticus and Numbers, it represented the very same Hebrew word which was represented by *ekklesia* in other books. (Numbers 16:3; Deuteronomy 23:2) This means that the two Greek terms were really synonyms. This is true even in the New Testament, where one writer used both terms in referring to a Christian congregation. (James 2:2; 5:14) In the first of these two verses, the King James version preserved the true meaning of the term *synagogue* by translating: "if a man . . . comes into your assembly." Nineteenth-century revisers pushed consistency too far by calling this Christian gathering "your synagogue," but they at least reminded English readers that the church is in fact the child of the synagogue.

The study of the Hebrew scriptures in their earliest surviving translation, the Bible of Greek-speaking Jews and early Christians, leads to a very significant conclusion. When such Jews called their meeting for worship a *synagogue* and when Christians called theirs an *ekklesia,* they meant exactly the same thing. Both Jews and Christians intended to claim direct historical continuity with the ancient congregation of the Lord, called out and gathered together in the Old Testament. In other words, Christians as well as Jews believed themselves to be inheritors of all the promises given by God in the covenant which he made with his chosen people, Israel. It is this idea of a covenant between God and his people which lies at the root of what we know as the Old and the New Testaments, for in reality it was the covenant which created and established the church.

Heirs of the Promises

The idea of community life ordered by mutual pledges of
fidelity was so common among the people of Israel that the term
covenant was used in a variety of ways. It could designate the
marriage vows exchanged between husband and wife. (Malachi
2:14) Or it might refer to a promise of allegiance made by subjects at the coronation of a new king. (II Kings 11:4-12) Or the
same word could be used to describe a treaty of peace between
rulers of two nations. (I Kings 20:34) Since it was regarded as
a serious offense to break such solemn promises, the Hebrew
scriptures emphasized the importance of keeping covenants.

By far the most frequent occurrence of this idea was in descriptions of the special relationship which God had established
with the people he had chosen. The essential moral quality of
this relationship was always faithfulness. The Lord himself was
described as "the faithful God who keeps covenant and steadfast
love with those who love him and keep his commandments."
(Deuteronomy 7:9) Even if his people were to forsake his law
and receive just punishment, God would never violate his covenant with them, nor alter his pledged word. (Psalm 89:30-34)
Consequently his promise was called an "everlasting covenant."
(Genesis 9:16; 17:19; Psalm 105:8-10)

Few stories in the Old Testament were of greater significance
to Judaism and early Christianity than the account of the covenant with Abraham, in which God promised to bless him and
his descendants, making him the father of many nations. (Genesis 15:5-6; 17:1-9) Since this promise was given when the pa-
triarch was very old and his wife still childless, it had seemed
almost too good to be true. Yet implicit throughout the story
ran the confidence that God could be depended upon to keep
his word. So Abraham believed God and his trust was accepted
as the basis of a right relation with God. In turn, he and his de-

scendants accepted the obligation to keep the covenant and to serve God as his faithful people.

The influence of this story and the different interpretations of its meaning are reflected in many parts of the New Testament. John the Baptist warned any Jews who relied too much on mere physical descent from Abraham, that God could fulfill his promise in other ways. (Matthew 3:9) Jesus predicted that many people would come from east and west to share with Abraham and his children in the blessings of God's reign. (Matthew 8:10-11) Paul pointed to the example of Abraham's faith to show that God's promise was not a reward which had to be earned, but a free and undeserved gift. (Romans 4:1-22; Galatians 3:6-9) A later Christian writer, wishing to re-emphasize the moral obligations of the covenant, called attention to Abraham's obedience or "works" without which, he insisted, faith is dead. (James 2:20-26) But the most significant point in the story of Abraham lay in the fact that the covenant made with a single individual was to include a whole community of people, and this community would extend far beyond the immediate relationships of family, tribe, or race. Through Abraham, God's blessings would embrace all the nations of the earth. (Genesis 18:18; Galatians 3:8) Ideally this should have made the congregation of Israel, the people of the covenant, a great missionary society.

Israel's obligation to keep God's covenant was a constant theme throughout the scriptures. After Moses had led the people out of their slavery to the Egyptians, he read to them, at the foot of Mount Sinai, the book of the covenant; and the entire congregation pledged themselves to obey the word of God. (Exodus 24:3-7) Later, the same procedure was repeated when the book of the law was read to the people during the reign of King Josiah. (II Kings 22:8-13; 23:1-3) As time went on there was a growing tendency to think of Israel's obligation primarily as a matter of obeying the law. This included the religious and moral duties laid down in the ten commandments. (Deuteronomy 4:13-14; 5:1-21) It was also held to involve the rite of circumcision, by which every male Jew could be distinguished from a Gentile or foreigner. The story of Abraham was rewritten to require circumcision as the "sign" that God's covenant was made with a people set apart from other nations. (Genesis 17:10-14) Other people could be admitted to the covenant only if they accepted this sign and the obligations to which it bound them. (Genesis 17:22-27; Exodus 12:43-48) By its covenant with God, Israel was forbidden to make covenants with the people of heathen nations, and to contract marriages with foreigners. For Israel was a "holy people," consecrated to the service of the Lord their God. (Deuteronomy 7:1-11) As we shall see, Israel's sense of holiness frequently conflicted with its sense of mission to the world, while prophetic voices kept both ideals alive until at last the new covenant was established.

A Holy Nation

The ideal of holiness was an essential characteristic of the church in the Old Testament. The term *holy* was sometimes used as if it were merely the opposite of unclean in a purely physical sense. (Leviticus 10:10; 11:41-45) More often the word was used to describe persons or things dedicated to the deity. Keeping the sabbath holy meant separating it from the ordinary occupations of other days. (Exodus 20:8-11) The place of sacrificial worship was called the holy place. (Exodus 28:29) Everything connected with the duties of Aaron and his descendants, the priests, was described as holy—their garments, the crown, and the oil used at their anointing. (Exodus 28:2; 29:6; 30:30-32)

Yet it was to the entire congregation, none of whom ever set foot inside the sanctuary, that God had made the promise: "If you will obey my voice and keep my covenant . . . you shall be to me a kingdom of priests and a holy nation." (Exodus

19:5-6) Eventually this promise was claimed for the Christian church in its entirety. (I Peter 2:9) The holiness of the congregation was closely related to the awful purity of God himself. (I Peter 1:16; Leviticus 11:45)

On the other hand, Isaiah's vision of the holy God led him to confess his own and his people's uncleanness. (Isaiah 6:1-8) One of the greatest contributions of the prophets had been the reinterpretation of the ideal of holiness to mean not merely ceremonial consecration, but moral qualities of righteousness and mercy. Where the law had said: "You shall be holy; for I the Lord your God am holy," Jesus was to say: "Be merciful, even as your Father is merciful." (Luke 6:36)

Yet the danger that sanctity would be defined too narrowly was a constant threat to Israel's mission to the world. It was easier to think of the vocation to be a congregation of saints as one that required separation from the rest of mankind. Fear of defilement through association with heathen people raised an invisible barrier between Jew and Gentile. It even led Jews who had gained a reputation for piety to separate themselves from others who seemed less meticulous about observing every detail of the law. Jesus found among such pious "separatists" a serious obstacle to his work among the people. The clash between their ideals and his own became sharp and clear in their criticisms of his dealings with sinners, and in his replies. (Mark 2:15-17; Luke 15:1-32; 18:9-14)

One of the noblest insights in the entire range of Hebrew scripture had been voiced by an unknown prophet of the exile, who preached that God had called Israel to be not only his servant, but a light to the nations, that his salvation might reach the ends of the earth. (Isaiah 42:1, 6; 49:3, 6-7) Even the dispersion of the Jews from their homeland could be seen as part of God's providential plan for the conversion of the nations. Another great prophetic insight declared that Israel and Judah themselves stood in need of repentance and forgiveness, for they had broken the covenant. But because God is merciful, Jeremiah could look forward to the day when God would make a new covenant with his people, not carved on tables of stone, but written in their hearts. (Jeremiah 31:31-34)

Later, Christian missionaries proclaimed that the fulfillment of this promise of a new covenant had come with the mission of Jesus. (II Corinthians 3:2-6) Here the King James version spoke of a "new testament." Since the English word *testament* generally refers to a man's last will, while the term *covenant* usually means a contract or agreement, it was difficult for the average reader of this older version to realize that both words were used to translate the same Greek term. The explanation of this apparent confusion can be found in the Septuagint, where the Greek term meaning a will or testament was used to translate the Hebrew word for covenant. Thus a Christian writer found it possible to play on the double meaning of the term. (Hebrews 9:15-20)

It has been alleged by some that the people of the Dead Sea Scrolls anticipated Christianity in all this, but the evidence of these documents hardly supports such a contention. Their *Manual of Discipline*, which contains the rules by which these people governed their community, indicates that they probably entered into a solemn renewal of the old covenant, year after year. Another work, believed to be closely related to the same sect, the "Damascus Document" discovered in Egypt in 1910, speaks of those who entered into a "new covenant." But there is no suggestion in either writing that the former covenant was in any way abrogated or abolished. On the contrary, study and practice of the law given through Moses was at the center of all that these people held most sacred.

The priests who presided over the council of this separated community near the shores of the Dead Sea emphasized strongly Israel's vocation to holiness. This in turn had brought them into a controversy with the temple hierarchy at Jerusalem which is of no immediate concern to us here. It is enough to observe that at the heart of the old covenant stood the ancient sacrificial system which the sacred scriptures prescribed, as it was believed to have been practiced since the days of Israel's wanderings in the wilderness. (Exodus 24:3-8) This too formed a prominent feature of the religious background from which the Christian church emerged.

Temple and Synagogue

The historic mission of Jesus was directed toward his own people, the Jews. Rarely did it bring him into personal relations with Gentiles. It was only later that his followers began to carry his message to people living beyond the geographical boundaries of their tiny homeland in Palestine. Thus the ultimate result of his life and teaching was to be a Christian missionary movement which would plant the church in the far corners of the earth. But before that could happen there were to be more immediate and more disturbing results. Jesus was to come into conflict with the religious and civil leaders of his nation, who would surrender him to the Roman governor of Judea for judgment and execution.

The chief leaders in the community of Israel at this time were the scribes and the priests. These two groups were closely identified with two great institutions which had been established as practical embodiments of the ideals of Israel, the synagogue and the temple.

The more ancient of these two was the temple located at Jerusalem, the national capital. Long before its erection, however, there existed the orders of priesthood to whom were assigned the duties of offering daily sacrifices to God. Although ideally the whole congregation was to be a kingdom of priests and a holy nation, one particular tribe descended from Levi had been consecrated to provide the ministry of the sanctuary.

During the days of Israel's nomadic wanderings from Egypt

to the promised land the holy place had been furnished in a large portable shelter, known as the tabernacle. But after the Israelites settled in Canaan, they adopted certain local shrines of the older heathen inhabitants as places in which to offer sacrifices to God—places like Beth-el and Gilgal.

Later, in the eighth century before Christ, life and worship in these so-called sanctuaries was still so deeply infected with heathen corruption that the prophets Amos and Hosea were inspired to condemn them. (Hosea 4:15-17; 12:11; Amos 3:14—4:5; 5:4-6) God, they insisted, is far more concerned about the righteousness of his people than he is about rites and ceremonies. (Hosea 6:6; Amos 5:21-24) Such protests prepared the way for a reformation which was carried out in the reign of King Josiah, about 620 B.C. The local, formerly heathen shrines were abolished, and the offering of sacrifices was from then on limited to a single central sanctuary. Although the laws in the book of Deuteronomy which authorized this reform did not specify the actual location of this single sanctuary, Jewish tradition always interpreted it to mean the temple at Jerusalem.

One important effect of these changes could hardly have been anticipated. During the sixth century before Christ, many Jews and their leaders were taken into exile from their homeland. Obedience to the Deuteronomic code made it impossible for the priests to offer sacrifices under such conditions. In Babylon, a Hebrew poet turned his thoughts to the temple on Mount Zion and lamented, "How shall we sing the Lord's song in a foreign land?" (Psalm 137:4) Yet it is inconceivable that for nearly fifty years those exiled Jews did not worship God at all. Their leaders seem to have solved the problem by devising a different form of service than that which was limited to the temple sanctuary.

The institution of the local synagogue probably owed its origin to this emergency. Its services, which consisted largely of instruction from the scriptures, were in no sense priestly. On the contrary, they provided the fullest possible opportunity for what may be called "lay" participation. Any male member of the congregation able to read the Hebrew scriptures was permitted to take his turn in doing so. It was in the normal capacity of a Jewish layman that Jesus read from the scroll of Isaiah in the assembly at Nazareth. (Luke 4:16)

According to the King James version of this story, when Jesus had finished this reading, "he closed the book, and he gave it again to the minister." This is apt to create a very inaccurate impression, since the person here referred to as a "minister" was not ordained to perform any peculiarly religious functions. In Aramaic he was called "servant of the congregation," actually the equivalent of sexton, or janitor. As caretaker of the synagogue building or "house of the congregation," his duties included bringing out, and putting away again, the rolls of scripture before and after each meeting for worship.

The scribes, or students of scripture, exercised their influence in the synagogue chiefly through the schools in which they taught, but except in the environs of Jerusalem few, if any of them, were members of the priestly families. In that sense they, too, were laymen.

The organization of the synagogue was simple and democratic. In each Jewish community a council of "elders" was elected by the congregation. This committee served as a local jury and also managed the financial affairs of the congregation including its charitable funds. There was a duly chosen chairman, who presided at meetings and appointed the particular members who were to read the scriptures or offer prayers on any given sabbath. This man was called "ruler of the synagogue." (Mark 5:22) All such officers were, of course, laymen. When members of the council laid their hands on the head of a newly elected elder, this action was merely the sign of their concurrence in the choice already made by the congregation. It did not constitute a form of "ordination," so much as a public acknowledgment of his lawful place among their number.

By the time of Jesus, synagogues had been organized in practically every town and village in Judea and Galilee, whereas the majority of the priests lived in or near Jerusalem within easy access to the temple. If, however, a priest happened to be present in some local synagogue, the chairman might invite him to conclude the service by pronouncing the blessing, known as the Aaronic benediction. (Numbers 6:22-26) However, this was never regarded as an essential part of the service, since in the absence of a priest it was simply omitted. Thus the custom provided an exception which proved the rule. The synagogue was always a lay organization.

The importance of this institution in the life of the Jewish people can hardly be overestimated. As a center of regular religious and moral instruction, it exerted a continuous influence on the daily life of all who attended its meetings. It offered hope that the prophetic ideal might become realized: "All your sons shall be taught by the Lord." (Isaiah 54:13; John 6:45) As a house of prayer for all the people, the synagogue was effective in ways that the temple at Jerusalem could not be. Attendance there was limited, at best, to occasional pilgrimages during the great annual festivals. On the other hand, the gospels record the the regular habit of Jesus, wherever he went in Galilee, of attending the local synagogue on the sabbath day, while the Acts report the continuation of the same practice by his disciples throughout the earliest period of Christian missionary expansion.

Just as Jesus accepted and used the synagogues of Galilee as the basis for his own mission to his people, so too when he was in Jerusalem, he apparently made frequent visits to the temple courts. (Mark 11:11, 15-19, 27-33; 12:35, 41—13:2; 14:49) During this period just before the Passover, he came into repeated conflict with the chief priests and other officials of the sanctuary, who eventually brought about his condemnation and death. Yet the evangelists indicate that Jesus was motivated by deeper reverence for the holy place and its worship than was to be found among its own ministers.

His protest against the sale of sacrificial animals and other commercial transactions within the sacred precincts is seen by one of the gospel writers as evidence of the zeal and devotion which Jesus felt toward the temple as his Father's house. (John 2:16-17) His own words indicate that this traffic may have taken place in the "court of the Gentiles," the one area of the temple enclosure open to non-Jews, who were thus deprived by the merchants of a place of worship there. They also hint that there may have been some degree of dishonest profiteering in the conduct of what was evidently a monopolistic business licensed by the priestly authorities. "Is it not written, 'My house shall be called a house of prayer for all the nations'? But you have made it a den of robbers." (Mark 11:17; Isaiah 56:7; Jeremiah 7:11) A more terrible indictment of a religious institution can scarcely be imagined, for it means the complete perversion of the very purpose for which the temple and its priesthood had been established.

By such words and actions as these, Jesus placed himself squarely in the succession of the prophets who had declared that sacrifices and ceremonies can never be an acceptable substitute for man's primary obligation to serve God by doing justice and showing mercy. (Isaiah 1:10-17; Jeremiah 6:20; Hosea 6:6; Amos 5:21-24) As Jeremiah had pronounced God's judgment on those who relied on the temple for their security, Jesus too is reported to have predicted the coming day of its destruction. (Jeremiah 7:1-14; Mark 13:1-2) Forty years later, during the last days of the Roman siege in A.D. 70, that prophecy was fulfilled. At the foot of the enclosure, known in Arabic as *Harem es-Sharif*, or "noble sanctuary," visitors to the old city of Jerusalem may still see all that remains of Herod's temple. Here lie those great foundation blocks which caused the disciples to exclaim, "Look, Teacher, what wonderful stones and what wonderful buildings!" But the spirit is departed from them, for the sanctuary is desolate.

The astonishing thing about all this is not that Jesus so accurately foresaw the course of future events, but that Jewish faith and worship survived the fall of the temple, without apparently losing what was then most vital to it. The explanation lies in the fact that the synagogue had already replaced the temple in the life of the people. In fact, it had freed them from captivity to an ancient belief that God's presence might be confined within one particularly sacred locality. The progress of the gospel of Jesus Christ from Jerusalem "to the end of the earth," which is the great theme of the Acts of the Apostles, shows that his disciples experienced the same liberation. That is the real significance of the words spoken to a woman of Samaria: "The hour is coming when neither on this mountain nor in Jerusalem will you worship the Father. . . . God is spirit, and those who worship him must worship in spirit and in truth." (John 4:21, 24)

This is not to say that Jewish worship as practiced in the temple had been totally lacking in spirit and reality. Since the time of Moses and the great prophets, the religion of Israel had increasingly recognized the uniqueness of God, his holiness, and righteousness. It was this recognition which set Judaism apart from all other religions of that time. But while the rejection of polytheism and idolatry marked a fundamental distinction between biblical religion and the variety of pagan cults flourishing in the Roman world, the continuance of animal sacrifices offered by the priests in the temple remained a mark of likeness to them. This whole system was a common feature of all worship in antiquity. It was what the average man understood and meant by "religion."

The organization of the temple hierarchy among the Jews differed only in detail from that in many other religions. The priesthood was strictly limited by family inheritance, though within the eligible families there were distinct gradations of rank. At the head stood the high priest, who at the time of Jesus was—rather ironically—a political appointee of the Roman governor of Judea. He alone entered the "holy of holies" once a year on the Day of Atonement. Below him, the rest of the priests took their turn in offering the daily sacrifices. Farther down the scale were the Levites, to whom were assigned a variety of functions, from the slaughtering of the sacrificial beasts to the singing of psalms and the playing of musical instruments. With such an ample retinue of attendants, the ceremonies of the temple could be conducted without convening an actual congregation of the people. Every adult male Jew, however, was expected to pay an annual half-shekel tax for the support of the temple, and of the various sacrifices offered by the priests on behalf of the people. This tendency toward worship by proxy, a common characteristic of all sacrificial cultus, was offset in Judaism by the institution of the synagogue. Its emphasis upon the regular gathering of the congregation, with fullest possible participation by its members, is one of the great Jewish inheritances of the church in the New Testament. Not only this, but members of the congregation were also instructed in the practice of offering prayer regularly in their own homes.

Religion in the Home

The ideal of addressing daily prayer and thanksgiving to God was fostered and kept alive in the hearts of the Jewish people by examples from the scriptures. (Daniel 6:10) Israel's great hymns of praise make frequent mention of such acts of devotion, particularly each morning and evening. (Psalms 1:2; 5:3; 55:17; 61:8; 86:3, 12; 92:1-2; 145:2) In the course of time the daily prayers came to include a recitation of the words:

> Hear, O Israel; The Lord our God is one Lord; and you shall love the Lord your God with all your heart, and with all your soul, and with all your might. (Deuteronomy 6:4-5)

The same passage in the Hebrew Bible also required faithful Jews to instruct their children in the obligations of their religion. (Deuteronomy 6:6-7, 20-25) In this way the public worship of the temple and the synagogue was supported by those habits of private prayer which the gospel records show to have been so characteristic of the life and teaching of Jesus. (Matthew 6:6; 7:7-11; Mark 1:35; 6:46; 14:32-38; Luke 11:1; 18:1)

There were, of course, some aspects of the activities connected with the temple in which the people were expected to take part, such as the observance of certain feasts and fasts. Chief among these were the Passover and the annual Day of Atonement. But here a further distinction must be observed. For example, the paschal lamb was offered as a sacrifice by the priests in the temple, but the Passover meal, consisting not only of the lamb, but the unleavened bread, the bitter herbs, the wine and other special dishes was eaten by Jewish families in their own private homes. There the service, which included a reading of the scriptural account of the exodus from Egypt, with praise and thanksgiving to God for his deliverance, was presided over by the head of the house, the father or the eldest brother.

Thus when the earliest Christians held their meetings for worship in private houses—chiefly for want of any other available place—they were following a very old and common Jewish custom. The Hebrew scriptures give evidence that the Passover meal had originated as a purely domestic celebration which could be observed wherever the people happened to dwell. (Exodus 12; Joshua 5:10-11) Its connection with the sanctuary at Jerusalem was a secondary development, resulting from the Deuteronomic reform undertaken at the time of King Josiah. (Deuteronomy 16:5-6; II Kings 23:9, 21-23)

In the course of time, other religious meals came to be observed in Jewish homes, although there was no specific provision for them in scripture. Such was the supper-time service known as the "hallowing" of the sabbath. The meal, like the day itself, began at sunset. Its simple service consisted chiefly of blessings, or prayers of thanksgiving, offered to God for having provided the day of rest, as well as the food about to be eaten, particularly the wine and the bread. At such Jewish home services, too, the head of the family read the scriptures and offered the prayers, with other members of the household participating in various ways.

Evidently similar meals played an important part in the life of the Jewish community whose rules have come to light in the Dead Sea Scrolls. However, the *Manual of Discipline* of this sect indicates that these were not actually domestic observances like the Passover, and the Hallowing of the Day. While there is still uncertainty whether or not members of this group were forbidden to marry, there is no specific mention of women or children in the *Manual*. The meals which it describes are clearly those of an association made up entirely of men, with at least one priest, who alone was authorized to offer the blessings for the bread and the wine.

It is not surprising that some students of these documents have suggested that they provide a possible pattern for the supper which Jesus shared with the twelve disciples in the upper room at Jerusalem. They point out that the gospel records, likewise, make no mention of the presence of women or children. But it is equally important to observe that it was not a priest, but Jesus himself, whether as the eldest or as the teacher, who broke the bread, took the cup, and gave thanks to God in this service. (Mark 14:17-26) It was Jesus, too, who said the blessings or thanksgivings at other evening meals with larger companies of his followers, among whom women and children are specifically mentioned by one evangelist. (Matthew 14:15-21; 15:32-38)

Later, in the early Christian community at Jerusalem, a meal of religious fellowship known as "the breaking of bread" was clearly differentiated from attendance at the temple, as a domestic observance eaten in homes of members of the congregation.

(Acts 2:42; 46-47) Although Paul drew certain analogies between this meal and Jewish, or even pagan sacrifices, he did not refer to the Lord's supper itself as a sacrifice. (I Corinthians 10:14-22) One of the later writers of the New Testament urged that since the complete self-offering of Jesus had established a new covenant, further sacrifices for sin were neither necessary, nor possible. (Hebrews 10) As if in warning against any drift toward reliance on worship by proxy, he exhorted his readers not to neglect to meet together—as had become the habit of some —but in the name of Jesus continually to offer up a sacrifice of praise to God, and to share their goods with others, an offering pleasing to God. (Hebrews 10:25; 13:15-16) This profound sense of fellowship among believers, in thanksgiving to God for his redemption through Jesus Christ, formed an essential characteristic of the church in the New Testament.

Baptism and Repentance

There was still another Jewish practice for which no directions had been given in scripture, but which was probably already in use at the time of Jesus. That was the baptism of Gentile converts, or proselytes. Laws in the book of Leviticus ordered any Jew who had contracted certain forms of uncleanness to purify himself by means of a ceremonial bath. Idolatry especially was a defilement from which such cleansing was required. (Ezekiel 36:25; 37:23) So it was natural to conclude that a convert from any of the pagan nations should undergo similar washing before he could become a member of the congregation of saints.

Such baptism of proselytes was in no sense a Jewish "sacrament," since it was not in itself the means whereby a Gentile entered into the commonwealth of Israel. The law prescribed circumcision as the outward "sign" of the covenant. Only by undergoing this rite could a non-Jewish male inherit the privileges, as well as the responsibilities, of membership in the people of God. But since no man could fulfill the duties of such membership without systematic instruction based on the scriptures, attendance at the weekly meetings of the synagogue was a prerequisite to the acceptance and baptism of proselytes.

Instruction and discipline—these were important characteristics of Judaism. Two centuries before Christ, Jeshua ben Sira, whose teachings are included in the *Apocrypha,* had invited young men to come to his house of instruction, or school. He urged them to submit to the "yoke," adding that after a little labor he had "found rest." (Sirach 51:23-30) Jesus spoke in similar terms, when he said: "Take my yoke upon you and learn from me, . . . and you will find rest for your souls." (Matthew 11:29) The sabbath rest from labor, which made possible the weekly meeting of the congregation to hear the word of God, provided opportunity for spiritual refreshment as well as physical relaxation. In this way it had a far deeper influence on the religious and moral character of the Jewish people than any of the more colorful pagan holidays ever had on the lives of Greeks or Romans. Men can only truly worship a God in whom they wholeheartedly believe, and such faith comes through the hearing of his word. (Romans 10:14-17)

The church in the New Testament could never have fulfilled its mission to the world if the apostles had not learned from Jesus to recognize the priority which must always belong to "the ministry of the word." (Acts 6:1-4) Their preaching, like that of their Master, began with a summons to repentance. (Mark 1:14-15; Acts 2:38) It was this act of turning from sin to God which gave meaning to baptism as an outward sign of inward purification of life. The best minds in Judaism had always taken the position that no external ceremony has any significance unless the heart of the worshipper is right. Scribes like Jeshua ben Sira continued to repeat the warnings of prophets like Isaiah, that God is not pleased with the offerings of the ungodly, nor can sin be expiated by a multitude of sacrifices. (Sirach 34:19; Isaiah 1:11)

In later rabbinic tradition, it is related that after the fall of the temple brought the ministry of the altar to an end, a certain Jewish student, viewing its ruins, lamented the destruction of the place where atonement had been made for Israel's sins. But his teacher corrected him, pointing out that God had said, "I desire mercy and not sacrifice." (Hosea 6:6) Other Jewish teachers, too, insisted that the essential thing on the Day of Atonement was not the sin offering, but repentance and confession of one's sins to God. This was held to be in full accord with the teaching of the Hebrew scriptures: "The sacrifice acceptable to God is a broken spirit; a broken and contrite heart, O God, thou wilt not despise." (Psalm 51:17) He does not require sacrifices and sin offerings, but desires men who delight to do his will. (Psalm 40:6-8) It is such profound insights into the heart of God which one of the later writers of the New Testament found revealed and fulfilled in the life and work of Jesus. (Hebrews 10:5-10)

This is a common theme in the New Testament, the continuity of the mission of Jesus with the long history of God's dealing with his people in the Old Testament. It is in fact a theme which takes us back to our starting point in the opening events of Mark's gospel. Before Jesus inaugurated his public teaching in the synagogue at Capernaum, Mark indicates that there had been a period of intense preparation. However, what he describes is not so much the personal training by which Jesus made ready to undertake his work, but rather the preparation of the people to receive the message of the gospel through the activity of a new prophetic messenger from God.

The Preparation of the Gospel

Mark began his short story of Jesus, not as a biographer might be expected to do, by telling the names of his parents, the place and date of his birth, or the schools he attended and the progress he made in youth. Instead, "the beginning of the gospel" is connected with a prophecy which all the later evangelists likewise believed was fulfilled in the work of John the Baptist. (Mark 1:3; Matthew 3:3; Luke 3:4; John 1:23) Probably every devout Jew was familiar with the words:

> A voice cries: 'In the wilderness prepare the way of the Lord.'
> (Isaiah 40:3)

The people of the Dead Sea Scrolls had applied this prophecy to their own retreat into the wilderness of Judea. In their *Manual of Discipline* they explained that this preparation of the Lord's way meant the study of the law which God had commanded through Moses, and the doing of all that the prophets had revealed through his holy Spirit.

The preparation which John proclaimed necessary was "a baptism of repentance for the forgiveness of sins." The Scroll people likewise required all who entered into their covenant to confess their sins. It is uncertain whether this was accompanied by a single rite like baptism. More likely they practiced ceremonies of purification which were repeated from time to time. Next, John announced the coming of a mightier one, explaining, "I have baptized you with water; but he will baptize you with the Holy Spirit." The *Manual* insists that it is only by a holy spirit disposed to unity in God's truth that a man will be cleansed from all his iniquities. But the Scroll people believed that this would not take place until the last times, at the season of God's visitation for judgment. Meanwhile, two spirits, one of truth and the other of error, were said to struggle for mastery in man's heart.

Fuller accounts of John's preaching in the later gospel records show that he too shared this expectation of a coming judgment, of which the "mightier" would be the agent. (Matthew 3:7-12; Luke 3:7-17) Such expectations regarding God's final overthrow of falsehood and evil are often described by the term "eschatology," from a Greek adjective *eschatos*, meaning "last." It means a doctrine of the last times. Popular Jewish eschatology usually included hope for the coming of the Messiah, the Anointed of the Lord. The Scroll people held a peculiar hope for the coming of an Anointed of Aaron (a priest) and an Anointed of Israel (perhaps a king), but this need not concern us. It is enough to recall that eschatological expectations, in a variety of forms, were part of the religious atmosphere of the people among whom the gospel was first proclaimed.

While the Scroll people still looked forward to an uncertain future, when God would cleanse mankind by a holy spirit, New Testament writers affirmed that this had already begun to take place, as the result of the coming of Jesus, the Messiah, or in Greek terms, the Christ. So Peter was to say of the later experience of the disciples at Pentecost, "This is what was spoken by the prophet Joel: 'And in the last days it shall be that I will pour out my Spirit upon all flesh.'" (Acts 2:16-17; Joel 2:28) No doubt that is why Mark called the baptism of Jesus, "the beginning of the gospel." For when Jesus came up out of the water, he saw the heavens rent apart, and the Spirit descending upon him, while a voice from heaven said, "Thou art my beloved Son; with thee I am well pleased." (Mark 1:9-11)

Everything that the Scroll people strove to attain seems to come to sharper focus in this initial event of the Gospel according to Mark. Yet there are very significant differences between the rest of the story of Jesus, and that of these people. The gospel begins where they began, but it does not stop there. In order to separate themselves from the habitation of wicked men, they went out into the wilderness, and there they stayed. Jesus remained in the wilderness only a few days—Mark speaks of forty —and then he went into Galilee. There, like John the baptizer, Jesus called on his people to repent.

Only, in the teaching of Jesus, this summons was accompanied by the promise that God's reign was at hand. That is the reason the message of Jesus is described as a gospel—good news from God. (Mark 1:14-15) Yet it was that very message which set the feet of Jesus squarely on the way that led him to his death on the Roman gallows which we call the cross. To his first disciples that was a shocking fact which, by all the logic of human reasoning, might well have brought his mission among them to a hopeless end. It was the surprising events which followed immediately after his crucifixion which united them ever more firmly together as a new community. For it was their faith in his resurrection which ultimately led to their separation from the ancient congregation of Israel, to become known in history to the present day as the church of Christ.

CHAPTER TWO

THE WAY CALLED
A SECT

AFTER a brief period of public teaching in Galilee, during which he gathered and trained a small company of disciples, Jesus went up to Jerusalem at the feast of the Passover. There the Sadducean priests quickly reached the conclusion that his teaching was endangering the nation and turned him over to Pontius Pilate, who sentenced him to die on a gallows as one who claimed to be the king of the Jews. Centuries of faith have transformed into a religious symbol this instrument of death on which condemned criminals were hanged in the Roman world. Indeed, between the Jewish and the Christian churches stands the cross.

The story is familiar to every reader of the New Testament. Yet the relation between these tragic events and the origin of the Christian church as a religious community, separate and distinct from Judaism, presents a perplexing problem. The death of Jesus not only failed to put an end to the movement of his disciples, but soon became the central theme of their faith and message. Within a few weeks after the crucifixion they were proclaiming to all who would listen that God had raised Jesus from the dead to exalt him as Messiah and Lord. (Acts 2:22-36)

This proclamation of the death and resurrection of Jesus Christ formed the central core of the gospel preached by all the apostles. For fully a generation it was transmitted chiefly in this oral form, before any of the later evangelists, beginning with Mark, attempted to set down more complete accounts in writing. The earliest written records of it which we have are preserved in letters of Paul, all sent to Christians who were already familiar with the primary facts. A notable example appears in the letter to the church at Corinth, in which the apostle reminded his readers of the message which he had already preached to them:

> I delivered to you as of first importance what I also received, that Christ died for our sins in accordance with the scriptures, that he was buried, that he was raised on the third day in accordance with the scriptures. (I Corinthians 15:3-4)

Then he proceeded to list the persons, most of them still living when he wrote, to whom the risen Jesus had appeared, concluding with the statement, "last of all . . . he appeared also to me."

When Paul, like the rest of the apostolic missionaries, said that Christ had died and had been raised from the dead "in accordance with the scriptures," he meant that these events fulfilled certain ancient prophecies of the Hebrew Bible. Thus, the gospel consisted of the personal testimony of witnesses, who spoke with the conviction born of experience. These men were confirmed in their faith by the evidence which they found in the sacred books of Judaism, to which they appealed for corroboration of the truth of their message. It was by such testimony that the earliest disciples, who had followed Jesus as learners in his "school," made their bid for recognition as a legitimate sect within the congregation of Israel, the people of God. It was important to demonstrate that the points which they held "as of first importance" were in accord with the law and the prophets, through which God had revealed his word. On this basis they might claim the right to teach their faith to others. For it was these important points with respect to the Messiah's death and resurrection which distinguished the gospel from doctrines and opinions held by the rest of their fellow Jews. The question naturally arises, how the

message proclaimed by the apostles was related to the one which
Jesus himself had preached.

The Reign of God

When Jesus began to preach in Galilee, the central theme of
his message was the sovereignty of God:

> The time is fulfilled, and the kingdom of God is at hand; repent,
> and believe the gospel. (Mark 1:15)

He had said nothing about the long-awaited reign of the Messiah,
nor had he mentioned the restoration to Israel of its national
sovereignty, twin hopes in the hearts of many Jews at that time.
Such hopes still dominated the minds of his closest followers
even after his crucifixion. (Acts 1:6) This persistent dream of
independence from foreign rule led to a popular confusion of
God's reign with an earthly kingdom, but its roots were deeply
embedded in the Hebrew scriptures. The gospel writers report
no instance in which Jesus defined precisely what he meant by
the kingdom of God, nor by another phrase sometimes substituted for it, "the kingdom of heaven." Instead, he illustrated his
meaning in parables or in comparisons between God's reign and
familiar circumstances in the life of his hearers.

The Hebrew scriptures often spoke of God as the king of Israel,
the real ruler of his people. (Psalm 149:2; Isaiah 43:14-15) It
was reported that when the elders of Israel had petitioned Samuel to give them a human king like other nations, the prophet
denounced their nationalistic ambitions as nothing less than the
rejection of God as their true sovereign. (I Samuel 8:4-7;
12:12) Whether this ideal of Israel as a theocracy or nation
governed immediately by God was ever realized or not, it was at
least clearly affirmed in the scriptures.

More than this. The growth of monotheistic faith in Israel
made it impossible to think of God's sovereignty as confined

within the borders of a single land, however holy. He is a great king who rules over all the nations. (Psalm 47:2, 7) Unlike the reign of a human monarch, God's reign is not limited to any passing era in history. So he is called not only "king of the nations" but also "everlasting king." (Jeremiah 10:7, 10) Ultimately the Lord will be acknowledged as the one rightful sovereign over all the earth. (Zechariah 14:9) He is a great king above all gods. In fact there are no gods beside him and his reign is universal, for heaven is his throne and the earth is his footstool. (Psalm 95:3; Isaiah 45:21-23; 66:1) Beyond this human thought and words could not go.

Unfortunately, the more familiar English versions of the Bible tend to create a false impression in the mind of the average reader when they speak of the "kingdom" of God. In modern English, this word has acquired a local association. More often than not it is used to describe a territory governed by some monarch, a country subject to a king. Biblical writers had no such spatial domain in mind when they spoke of God's kingdom. What they meant was his kingship, his royal authority and right to rule. A more accurate translation of their affirmations would be: "His sovereignty rules over all" and "his reign is an everlasting reign." (Psalms 103:19; 145:13; Daniel 4:3)

The same thing is true in the teaching of Jesus. When he used the expression usually translated "the kingdom of heaven," he did not mean a realm located in the sky. On the contrary, he taught his disciples to pray that God's reign might come and his will be done on earth as well as in heaven. (Matthew 6:10) However, he followed a pious practice common among the Jews, who often substituted the word "heaven" for the holy and unutterable name of God. Thus to "swear by heaven" was simply a way of avoiding the invocation of the divine name when taking an oath, just as to "sin against heaven" meant to commit an offense against God. (Matthew 5:34; Luke 15:18) Other words sometimes substituted for the name of God in the gospel records are "the Blessed" and "the Power." (Mark 14:61-62) So the phrase "kingdom of heaven" meant exactly the same as "kingdom of God," that is, his sovereignty or reign.

Some interpreters of the gospels contend that when Jesus announced "the kingdom of God is at hand," he meant that it had actually arrived. They point to his further statement that it had "come upon" the people to whom he spoke. (Matthew 12:28; Luke 11:20) From such evidence, they conclude that Jesus taught a "realized eschatology," claiming that the final triumph of God's sovereignty was already being accomplished in his own mission. Thus the long-expected "last times" had already begun. Many New Testament scholars reject this explanation. Yet there may be an element of truth in it which can be grasped by paying careful attention to the occasion on which Jesus is reported to have asserted that God's reign had overtaken his critics.

At that time certain types of illness, particularly mental illness, were popularly explained by saying that the sick person was "possessed by a demon" or an evil spirit. The first three gospels all record that on one occasion, after Jesus had restored such a person to his right mind, his opponents charged, "He casts out demons by Beelzebub, the prince of the demons." In reply to this accusation, Jesus had asked, "If Satan is divided against himself, how will his kingdom stand?" (Luke 11:14-18; Matthew 12:22-26) So far the story follows closely the record of the earliest evangelist, except that Mark quoted Jesus as saying that Satan's reign was "coming to an end." (Mark 3:22-26) The downfall of Satan was usually connected with the triumph of God's reign. So it was appropriate for the later evangelists to report at this point another saying of Jesus: "If it is by the Spirit of God that I cast out demons, then the kingdom of God has come upon you." Luke used the phrase "by the finger of God," but the wording in Matthew suggests that the renewed activity of the Holy Spirit furnished evidence that the "last times" had already begun.

While such sayings reflect clearly the inner assurance of Jesus that his mission had the approval and enabling power of God himself, they provide no evidence that he identified the reign of God with the growing company of his own followers. It was only at a later date that some of his parables about the "kingdom" came to be understood with reference to the church and its missionary expansion in the world—parables such as those about the leaven, the mustard seed, the weeds among the wheat, and the fishing net. (Matthew 13:24-43; 47-50) But Jesus could scarcely have expected any one to understand these stories in that way, long before the Christian church could be recognized as distinct from the old congregation of Israel. Nor is there any reason to think this was their original meaning.

We cannot hope to come to a proper understanding of the teaching of Jesus about the coming of God's reign, by demanding that it furnish answers to questions that had not yet arisen when he spoke. People sometimes ask whether Jesus taught that God's reign is already present in human history, or only to be manifested in some future "beyond history." Or again, whether it is "this-worldly" or purely "other-worldly," an "objective reality" or an "inward state." But such antitheses and dilemmas are modern inventions to which the battle of proof texts can give no conclusive answer. Nor need we attach too much importance to the often debated problem: did Jesus say, "the kingdom of God is within you," (following the translation of 1611) or "in the midst of you"? (Luke 17:21)

One of the most complicated questions in modern gospel study is how far Jesus actually shared the popular eschatological hopes that animated the imagination of many of his first hearers. The answers given by various scholars, often equally competent, tend to differ according to the way in which they attempt to combine, balance, or contrast certain apparently conflicting pictures which may be drawn from the vivid imagery of the gospels. For example, the records indicate that Jesus did share the expectation of a time when the dead would rise to new life with God, a life different from life in this world, though no less real. (Mark 12:18-27) But the reports of his words do not specifically connect that belief with the "coming" of God's reign, or with men's "entering" it.

Likewise, in the story of the coming of the Son of man, where the righteous are invited to come and inherit "the kingdom prepared for you from the foundation of the world"; although the scene is laid in the future, nothing is said about the resurrection as a prelude to the judgment and entrance into that kingdom. (Matthew 25:31-46) Still another story speaks of the torments suffered in Hades (the abode of the dead) by a rich man who failed to help a poor man lying at his gate. Yet its main purpose is to warn against a popular belief that if someone should return from the dead, the wicked would repent: "If they do not hear Moses and the prophets, neither will they be convinced if some one should rise from the dead." (Luke 16:31) No doubt the apostolic preachers had discovered the truth of those words from their own experience in proclaiming the gospel of Christ's resurrection.

According to Mark, Jesus had spoken of the advent of God's reign as something that would fall within the experience of some of his immediate hearers. "There are some standing here who will not taste death until they see the kingdom of God come with power." (Mark 9:1) Luke's record of this statement does not substantially alter its meaning by omitting the last three words. (Luke 9:27) Another version speaks of seeing "the Son of man coming in his kingdom." (Matthew 16:28) As the first disciples died, one after another, the question must have arisen how such a saying might be interpreted, lest the hopes it had aroused be dashed to disappointment. That the preaching of the gospel, by which the church made its way across the world, was accompanied "with power" was a fact often testified in the New Testament. (Acts 4:33; Romans 15:18-19; I Corinthians 2:4-5; I Thessalonians 1:5) In response to the question of the disciples, "Will you at this time restore the kingdom to Israel?" the risen Lord had promised, "You shall receive power when the Holy Spirit has come upon you; and you shall be my witnesses . . . to the end of the earth." (Acts 1:6-8) Yet it was remembered that Jesus had warned that the kingdom of God would not come by signs to be observed, so that anyone could say, "Lo, here it is!" (Luke 17:21)

A comprehensive study of the teaching of Jesus about the reign of God, illuminated by the highest insights of the Hebrew prophets, suggests that we are not compelled to any final choice between mutually exclusive interpretations of its full significance. It is difficult to believe that anyone brought up on the scriptures as Jesus was could have thought of God's reign as existing only far off in some other sphere which men cannot enter until they die. Nor, on the other hand, could he have supposed that the sovereignty of God would be fully realized in any human society on earth, not even in the community of his own followers. Yet Jesus did teach his disciples not only to pray that the Father's will may be done on earth, but to make his righteous reign their first aim in life. (Matthew 6:10, 33)

The Crisis of God's People

Because God is the only true sovereign of his people, the prophets condemned disobedience to his righteous will as nothing less than rebellion. Such condemnations always fell most heavily, not on heathen nations ignorant of the word of the Lord, but on Israel. Again and again the nation was summoned before God's judgment seat and indicted as a rebellious people. (Isaiah 1:2-5; Jeremiah 4:11-17; Hosea 13:16)

The congregation of Israel was never specifically called the kingdom of God in scripture. For the church, like the nation, was made up of and governed by erring human members who failed both individually and collectively to fulfill the ideal of a people, holy to the Lord their God. His reign was always above the church, which was continually subject to his just judgment as well as his merciful correction. This is equally true in the New Testament. In true prophetic spirit, one writer, during a time when the Christian community was undergoing a fiery trial of persecution, declared that the time had come for judgment to begin with the household of God. (I Peter 4:12-17)

Although Jesus had begun his mission as a teacher in the synagogue, he spoke of himself as a prophet, and it was as a prophet that many of his hearers regarded him. (Mark 6:4, 15; 8:28; Matthew 21:11; Luke 7:16; 24:19) Yet such an opinion ran contrary to the belief generally accepted by Jews at that time, that the age of prophecy had ceased and that divine inspiration was a thing of the past. (Psalm 74:9) That is why the gospel writers all attached such great significance to the story that when Jesus was baptized, the Spirit of God descended upon him and God spoke to him as a father speaks to his son. (Mark 1:10-11; Matthew 3:16-17; Luke 3:21-22; John 1:32-34)

People's astonishment at the teaching of Jesus arose because they detected in it a ring of divine authority which contrasted sharply with the traditional instruction given by the scribes. As accredited interpreters of the scriptures, the scribes claimed the right to be heard on all questions dealing with the requirements of the divine law. But they based their authority on what had been said in the past, repeating as legal precedents the opinions of their own teachers before them. Compared with this, the message of Jesus struck his disciples as sounding a fresh note of urgency and expectation.

The historical situation of the Jewish community at the time of Jesus presented its leaders and people with a crisis of deepest national and religious importance. The times called for decisive action if Israel was to fulfill the purposes to which it was called by God. In terms of economic or political power this tiny country then subject to the mightiest empire on earth could not hope to be great. But in terms of service to God and the human spirit a higher form of greatness was possible. (Mark 10:42-45) As the servant of the Lord, Israel might still become "the light of the world." If only its people would let their true light shine in good deeds, men would come to glorify their Father in heaven. (Matthew 5:14-16) Jesus is reported to have spoken these words to his disciples, but at that time they were still active members of the Jewish community and what he said to them he intended for all.

What the crisis of that time required of the Jewish people was a radical reformation of their entire way of life, beginning at its central core. The gospel writers called this a "change of mind." That is the literal meaning of the Greek word usually translated as "repentance." The Hebrew prophets had expressed the same idea by saying that Israel must "turn" away from evil and "return" to the Lord. (Isaiah 31:6; Jeremiah 3:12-14; Ezekiel 18:30-32)

It would be a mistake to suppose that when Jesus called his hearers to repent or change their minds, he desired only an inward deepening of individual piety, rather than a far-reaching reformation of their community life as well. If that had actually been the case, it would have meant that even before he began his mission, Jesus had already given up the congregation of Israel, the Jewish church of his day, as hopelessly beyond redemption. There is not the slightest evidence in the gospel records that Jesus held any such pessimistic view of his nation. Nor is there any reason to suppose that from the beginning of his work Jesus expected only a small minority of the people to respond to his message, or that he had no hope that their official leaders might show some change of heart.

Jesus began his teaching in the synagogues going from town to town throughout Galilee. Later he extended its scope by preaching in the public courtyards of the temple at a time when large crowds were gathered in the national capital. These facts indicate that he always had in mind the widest possible appeal to his people. Yet he was well aware that the gateway to destruction is wide and the gateway to life is so narrow and difficult that few are able to find it. (Matthew 7:13-14) Among the prophetic books hope for the nation was sometimes so far reduced that it was said only a "remnant" would return to the Lord. (Isaiah 10: 20-22) In fact it was to such a saved remnant of Israel that the promise of a new covenant had been made. (Jeremiah 31:7-11, 31-34) Yet in the entire New Testament direct references to this idea of the faithful remnant occur in only one book. (Romans 9:27; 11:5) Jesus evidently made no mention of it, even when he was asked whether those who are saved would be few. (Luke 13:23) Any limitation which may have existed, therefore, lay not in the aim of Jesus, but in the response made by his hearers.

Perhaps the greatest limitation was to be found in the misunderstanding and opposition with which his teaching was met on the part of the official leaders of the Jewish church. The gospel records show Jesus in frequent controversy with the scribes. These debates were chiefly concerned with some point in the traditional interpretation of the law. Often they arose out of criticisms directed against Jesus or his disciples for failure to observe with scrupulous care rules about fasting, the sabbath rest, or ceremonial purification. (Mark 2:15-3:6; 7:1-8) In the eyes of the gospel writers such controversies appeared as a revival of the ancient struggle between upholders of religious formalism and a new prophetic voice declaring, as Hosea had done: "I desire mercy and not sacrifice." (Matthew 9:13; 12:7; 23:23)

Even if records of such controversies were colored by later debates between Christians and Jews over the relative authority of the law and the gospel, there was undoubtedly a solid core of historical fact behind them. The message of Jesus has never been more seriously misunderstood than by those who have tried to find in it a "new law." It was as a prophet, not as a legislator, that Jesus contrasted what had been said in ancient times with the challenging moral demands of God's reign. As a prophet, not a law-giver, he summoned men to imitate the perfection of God's mercy by meeting even their enemies in a spirit of love and forgiveness. As a prophet, too, he promised a place in God's reign to the poor in spirit, the peacemakers, and those who are persecuted for righteousness' sake. (Matthew 5:3-12; 43-48)

The collection of his teachings in which these words of Jesus were preserved closes with a solemn warning to his hearers. Like so much of his teaching, it was presented in the form of a story, the parable of two builders. In it Jesus compared every one who hears his words and does them to a wise man who built his house upon a rock as its foundation. When the winter storms brought floods, this house weathered the crisis unshaken. But to hear the words of Jesus, yet not do them, is to be like a foolish man who built his house on the sand, without adequate foundation. When the winds and floods beat against that house, it fell, and the ruin of that house was great. (Matthew 7:24-27; Luke 6:46-49)

The gospel records suggest that it was the same sense of urgency which had animated the mission of the great prophets of Israel that impelled Jesus to seek out the people of his day wherever they might be found. That he is reported to have avoided the kind of notoriety which might have come to him as a healer should not mislead us to suppose that Jesus deliberately limited his appeal to a small circle of select hearers, avoiding opportunities to reach a larger hearing. On the contrary, even if we allow for possible exaggeration on the part of enthusiastic followers, there is no reason to doubt that he often spoke to crowds that may have numbered several thousand people. We need, therefore, to give some attention to the appeal which Jesus made to the masses of men which the gospel writers describe as "the multitudes."

Jesus and the Multitudes

His controversies with the scribes afford no evidence that Jesus openly broke off relations with the synagogue. The most that the gospel records suggest is a shift in the scene and method of his teaching, as he found more responsive hearers elsewhere. This is indicated by the stories of large crowds of people who gathered to listen to him along the shore of the lake or in the open country. (Mark 4:1; 6:34) Once, in answer to especially caustic criticism, he had bluntly asserted that neutrality toward his mission was impossible, although hostility was to be expected: "He that is not with me is against me, and he who does not gather with me scatters." (Matthew 12:30; Luke 11:23) Probably few who heard that reply needed to be reminded of similar prophetic complaints against earlier leaders of Israel—that they had scattered God's flock whom he sought to gather again into their folds. (Jeremiah 23:1-4; Ezekiel 34:5-16)

In such a pastoral role of seeking and gathering together the scattered people, the gospel writers described the mission of Jesus to the unchurched multitudes of his day. In spite of the growing effectiveness of the synagogue as a place of religious instruction, large numbers of people remained unreached by it. Probably few of the learned men of the community felt the obligation to seek them out, as Jesus did. Because such people remained ignorant of the scribal interpretation of the law, stricter Jews like the Pharisees assumed that they did not really obey the law. They referred to the uneducated masses as "people of the land," a term which the scriptures had applied to heathen inhabitants of Palestine in the period after the exile. (Ezra 9:1-2, 11; 10:11) Thus such people, although Jews by birth, were regarded as little better than Gentiles.

It was this attitude toward the "people of the land" which prompted the frequent criticism that Jesus ate with "publicans and sinners." (Mark 2:13-17; Luke 15:1-2) For these "publicans" were Jewish tax collectors employed by the Roman government, while the word "sinner" was broadly used for anyone who did not strictly observe the law. The latest of the gospel records quotes as a Pharisean estimate of such people: "This crowd, who do not know the law, are accursed." (John 7:49) This may seem unusually harsh, yet even Hillel, one of the more liberal Jewish scholars of Jesus' day, said of the people of the land: "No ignorant man is pious."

Of course, Jesus did not share such opinions or he could not have associated so freely with "publicans and sinners." But he seems to have looked upon their lack of religious instruction as pitiable. When a great throng followed him into the country, it is reported "he had compassion on them, because they were like sheep without a shepherd; and he began to teach them many things." (Mark 6:34) The evangelist who wrote these words obviously had in mind the statement that Moses had appointed Joshua as the leader of the people in order that the congregation of the Lord might not become such a shepherdless flock. (Numbers 27:17) Jesus himself told a parable, in defense of his association with "sinners," about a shepherd who left a large flock safe in the fold to go in search of a single lost sheep and when he found it, brought it home rejoicing. (Luke 15:1-7) And according to one report, it was for a mission to "the lost sheep of the house of Israel" that he prepared and sent out twelve of his disciples. (Matthew 10:6)

If Jesus carried on his later work in a different setting, the central theme of his message remained constant—trustful dependence on God's sovereign rule. The heathen nations of the world were anxiously striving to establish their own material security, pathetically ignorant of the heavenly Father who knows and provides for the needs of his people, if only they seek his righteous reign. "Fear not, little flock, for it is your Father's good pleasure to give you the kingdom." (Luke 12:30-32)

The kingdom! It is a tragic paradox, yet scarcely surprising, that this word had power to awaken among the followers of Jesus memories of a dangerous dream of Jewish dominion over the world. This false hope had received encouragement from a book written during an earlier period of national crisis, the book of Daniel. In the seer's strange vision, four great beasts symbolized a succession of foreign empires which had oppressed Israel. In the judgment scene that followed, God was pictured as "one that was ancient of days," while Israel—in contrast to the beastlike forms—appeared as "one like a son of man." Puzzling as this vision seems to the average reader, the author of the book interpreted its meaning with startling clarity:

> The kingdom and the dominion and the greatness of the kingdoms under the whole heaven shall be given to the people of the saints of the Most High; their kingdom shall be an everlasting kingdom, and all dominions shall serve and obey them. (Daniel 7:27)

In other words, Israel's national sovereignty would not only be restored but extended over the whole earth, and since it was to last forever it would be equal in scope with the reign of God himself! (Daniel 4:3, 34; 6:26) A dangerous dream indeed!

How did Jesus fit into this dream in the minds of the multitudes? According to one late record, he had reason to believe that the people were planning to take him by force and make him king, so he left them and retired into the hill country alone. (John 6:15) If that ever was their intention, they must have become discouraged over their apparent abandonment by their leader. However, the earlier gospel records hardly suggest that the crowds regarded Jesus as a potential king, the captain of a revolt against Roman rule.

The familiar story of the events in the neighborhood of Caesarea Philippi indicates that it was one of his own immediate disciples who first expressed such a fantastic hope. On the road, Jesus had asked them: "Who do men say that I am?" Various

THE WAY CALLED A SECT 53

popular speculations about him were quoted in reply, but these all amounted to the same thing—the people regarded Jesus as a prophet. He was a particularly great prophet, to be sure—perhaps John the Baptist raised from the dead, or even Elijah, whose return was expected before the terrible day of judgment. (Malachi 4:5) In any case, men were calling Jesus an inspired messenger from God. Then came the second question: "But who do you say that I am?" Peter, apparently voicing the opinion of the rest, answered: "You are the Christ." (Mark 8:27-29)

What was the response of Jesus to this assertion of his messiahship, as preserved in the earliest account of it? From ancient times the evangelist Mark was said to have been the interpreter of Peter himself, in which case he must have told the story as that disciple remembered the event. Far from commending Peter for this attempt to clothe his teacher with the purple robes of royalty, Jesus instantly rebuked him, and warned all the disciples that they must not tell anyone about it. Already he had begun to foresee that the official leaders of the nation would reject his message, and even that death was threatening. Yet he thrust aside Peter's suggestion that he might easily escape this danger, as a temptation of the devil: "Get behind me, Satan! For you are not on the side of God, but of men." (Mark 8:27-33) That was Jesus' opinion of the nationalistic ambitions which so often characterized popular expectations of the Messiah.

Jesus had to repeat his rebuke on the night of his arrest, although accounts vary considerably as to the exact words he spoke. One of the disciples—it may have been Peter, as the fourth evangelist asserted—drew a concealed weapon and struck one of the servants of the high priest. But Jesus is reported to have said: "Put your sword back into its place." Then he went on: "All who take the sword will perish by the sword." (Matthew 26:52) Or else: "Shall I not drink the cup which the Father has given me?" (John 18:11) A third account has simply: "No more of this!" (Luke 22:51) Uncertainty about the precise words permits no doubt about the intention of Jesus. He refused to accept any defense of his person or his cause by violence and bloodshed.

Does this mean that Jesus likewise refused all recognition as Messiah, the Lord's Anointed? In the story of the investigation of his activities by the high priest and his legal advisors, the question is said to have been put to Jesus directly: "Are you the Christ, the Son of the Blessed?" Here, too, there is uncertainty regarding his reply. The earliest account is that he answered: "I am." (Mark 14:62) But later records seem to correct this. (Matthew 26:64; Luke 22:70) The words: "You have said so" or "You say that I am," are very ambiguous. Yet no more so than the reply which Jesus made to Pilate's question: "Are you the king of the Jews?" (Mark 15:2) It is inconceivable that Jesus could have claimed kingship in any sense which this Roman official would have attached to that word. Yet all accounts agree on one point. When Jesus was nailed to the cross, the accusation above his head contained the phrase "the King of the Jews." (Matthew 27:37; Mark 15:26; Luke 23:38; John 19:19)

Whatever statement Jesus may have made to the high priest about being the Messiah, the first three gospel records follow it with another: "You will see the Son of man sitting at the right hand of Power, and coming with the clouds of heaven." No one familiar with the Hebrew scriptures could miss the reference to Daniel. But in the centuries since that book was written, the meaning of the vision had been reinterpreted by other seers who thought of "the Son of man" as a heavenly being who would descend to earth on the last day to judge the world. Thus the figure, which in Daniel served as a symbol of the congregation of Israel, came to be thought of as an individual agent of God, sometimes called his chosen one, or his anointed. Yet in spite of the fact that this heavenly Messiah was called "Son of man," no one could have thought of him as a human being. He was always

described as possessing supernatural powers, such as usually belong to the angels in biblical thought. And although he was referred to as Messiah, he was never identified with the long expected king of David's line.

According to the gospel records Jesus had often spoken of
"the Son of man," and the evangelists seem to have believed that
he used the term in reference to himself. Thus they saw claims of
Messianic power in his statements: "the Son of man has authority on earth to forgive sins" and "the Son of man is Lord even of
the sabbath." (Mark 2:10, 28) But in the Hebrew scriptures
the words "son of man" always meant simply a human being.
(Psalm 8:4; 146:3) So there is no reason to suppose that the
original hearers of Jesus understood such sayings as a claim that
he was the Messiah. However, when he said: "the Son of man
must suffer many things," his disciples seem to have realized that
he meant that he himself must suffer. The idea that the Messiah
could suffer or die was so contradictory to all expectations that
they were entirely unprepared to accept it.

The gospel records present the faith of the early church concerning Jesus in his future role as judge of the living and the dead.
But that faith had to await his resurrection and the revelation of
the lordship to which God exalted him. Meanwhile, Jesus stood
before his human judges and was sentenced to death on a gallows. Thus the Christ was crucified, and those who governed
Palestine confidently expected that his followers would swiftly
disperse. One more potential threat to the Roman peace had
passed into oblivion. So it seemed, for a while.

Tacitus, the earliest Roman historian to mention Christianity,
said in the fifteenth book of his *Annals*:

> Christ, the founder of this denomination, was executed in the reign
> of Tiberius, by the procurator Pontius Pilate. Checked for a while,
> the fatal superstition broke out again, not only in Judea where the
> evil originated, but also at Rome.

However, Tacitus was not particularly concerned with the origin of this new sect, but rather with the peculiar circumstances connected with the great fire in the imperial capital in A.D. 64. In order to divert suspicion that he himself had ordered the conflagration, the emperor Nero had accused Christians of the crime and condemned them to death as enemies of the state. Although Tacitus felt no sympathy for the adherents of this "fatal superstition" as he called it, he broadly hinted his doubt that they were really guilty of the act with which Nero charged them. On the other hand, he lamented the fact that there had arisen a wave of popular pity toward these people who had been destroyed, as he said, "not as a public service, but to satisfy the cruelty of one man."

It is significant that while Tacitus had sufficient information about the Christians at Rome to trace the origin of their name to Christ, he was apparently unaware of the meaning of that name. At least he failed to give any reason for the action of the Roman governor of Judea in putting Christ to death. Yet the gospel writers all record that it was on the accusation of claiming to be the Messiah or king of the Jews that Jesus was crucified under Pontius Pilate. Had Tacitus understood that, it would have been more natural for him to have described Christianity as a revolutionary political movement, rather than a "fatal superstition." Nevertheless, he was right on the main point. Christians were members of a religious movement which originated among the Jews.

The Sect of the Nazarenes

Before the disciples of Jesus came to be regarded by outsiders as followers of a new religion, they had been thought of simply as adherents of a Jewish sect. Evidence of this earlier view is preserved in the Acts of the Apostles, in the account of Paul's defense before Felix, the Roman governor of Syria. A group of

Jewish leaders, headed by the high priest Ananias, had accused Paul of being an agitator among the people. In the words of the Jewish spokesman, Tertullus, he was "a ringleader of the sect of the Nazarenes." To this Paul replied:

> But this I admit to you, that according to the Way, which they call a sect, I worship the God of our fathers, believing everything laid down by the law or written in the prophets, having a hope in God which these themselves accept, that there will be a resurrection of both the just and the unjust. (Acts 24:14-15)

In other words, Paul claimed to be a faithful Jew, holding many beliefs held by other Jews.

In a later defense before Festus and King Agrippa, Paul mentioned his former adherence to what he called "the strictest party" or sect among the Jews, the sect of the Pharisees. (Acts 26:5) This meant that by coming to faith in Jesus Christ, Paul had transferred his allegiance from one Jewish sect to another, namely, the one which Tertullus referred to as "the sect of the Nazarenes." That is the usual English version of the Greek phrase used by Luke. However, if translators were consistent they would spell the name of this sect *Nazorees*, exactly as they say elsewhere "the sect of the Sadducees," or "the sect of the Pharisees." (Acts 5:17; 15:5)

The difficulty of connecting either *Nazoree* or *Nazarene* with the village called Nazareth is widely recognized among biblical scholars. In the Greek text of the earliest gospel record, the name of Nazareth is mentioned only once. (Mark 1:9) Everywhere else in that text, where the usual English versions refer to "Jesus of Nazareth," the Greek has either "Jesus the Nazarene" or "Jesus the Nazoree." (Mark 1:24; 10:47; 14:67; 16:6) Although the evangelist gave no clue to the origin or meaning of either term, in each case it seems to be used as a title with special religious significance. An attempt to connect it with the Hebrew *Nazirite,* which the Septuagint sometimes translated as "holy one," is not entirely satisfactory. If correct, it would explain why Jesus "the Nazarene" was also called "the holy one of God." (Mark 1:24)

One of the later gospel writers tried to connect the residence of Jesus' family at Nazareth with a prophecy: "He shall be called a Nazarene." (Matthew 2:23) This statement has long puzzled scholars, since the exact words are not to be found in the Hebrew scriptures, where the name of Nazareth was never mentioned. One possible solution may be that here the term *Nazoree* represents a Hebrew word meaning "branch," found in the prophecy of the prince who was to spring from the stock of Jesse, the father of David. (Isaiah 11:1) If that were so, it would account for the fact that a blind man at Jericho, on hearing Jesus spoken of as *Nazoree*, called him "son of David." (Mark 10:47) This in turn would mean that in the case before Felix, Paul was accused of being a leader of a sect made up of followers of the Branch, the long expected king of David's line.

One thing appears clear. After his death the disciples of Jesus were regarded by their fellow Jews as a sect or association holding certain peculiar beliefs by which they were distinguished from the adherents of other parties. In the King James version, Paul was quoted as referring to "the way which they call heresy." (Acts 24:14) This is somewhat misleading. No doubt other Jews did regard the claim of these "Nazarenes" that Jesus is the Messiah as a false doctrine. Yet there was enough freedom in Judaism to permit including within the congregation of Israel people who held a variety of views. Nevertheless, the new sect was widely spoken against. (Acts 28:22)

Sects invariably begin as the result of some failure on the part of an established church, often as an attempt to reform the church from within. At the time with which the book of Acts deals, the disciples of Jesus still entertained the hope that they might persuade the rest of their fellow Jews to follow "the Way." This term, sometimes with fuller descriptions such as "the way of salvation" or "the way of the Lord," was one of the earliest descriptions of the beliefs and teachings of "the sect of the Nazarenes." (Acts 9:2; 16:17; 18:25-26) It is a characteristically Jewish term. The oral interpretation of the law, sometimes called "the tradition of the elders," was known in Hebrew as *halakah*. That means a way or course of conduct, a rule by which to walk.

The disciples of Jesus believed that through his life and teaching God had revealed to them the way that leads to eternal life. Ultimately they held that Jesus himself is the way, the truth, and the life and that no one can come to the Father except through him. (John 14:6) Their sharpest differences with other Jews arose from the claims which they made for their Master, but it extended to many details of daily conduct and religious practice. Thus the followers of the Way came into frequent conflict with the official guardians of the established order in Jerusalem. Before we can speak of anything which may rightly be called the history of the Christian church, we have to take into account the struggles of a new sect among the Jews to maintain its very existence and the right to be different from other Jews. Moreover, before we can see the distinctive convictions of those earliest "Nazarenes" in their true perspective, we need to know something about the particular positions occupied by some of the other Jewish sects with whom they frequently found themselves in open controversy.

The Right to be Different

The earliest attempt to compile a historical account of these struggles of the disciples of Jesus to maintain their unique faith and way of life was made by the Greek Christian who wrote the Gospel according to Luke and the Acts of the Apostles, probably about A.D. 90. Luke's primary purpose seems to have been the instruction of his fellow Christians. Yet it is possible that he had in mind a second audience and aim. He addressed each of his two volumes to some one whom he courteously called "most excellent Theophilus." (Luke 1:3) Since this Greek name means "lover of God," it could have been intended as a symbolic reference to any Christian reader. But the word translated "most excellent" is practically a title, which Luke used three times in his second volume, always with the name of a Roman official of high rank. (Acts 23:26; 24:3; 26:25) In the last case it was Paul, making his defense in court, who addressed his words to the governor of Syria: "most excellent Festus."

Thus it is quite possible that Theophilus also may have been a Roman official who in the line of public duty found it necessary to investigate the beliefs of "the sect of the Nazarenes." When Luke said that he wrote that Theophilus might know the truth of the things of which he had been "informed," he used a Greek word which implied that the information had been given by word of mouth. While this could refer to the "catechetical" instruction given to Christian converts, it might apply to accusations and pleas for defense delivered orally in a court of law. Much of Luke's work was devoted to the explanation of differences which caused conflicts between the disciples of Jesus and other Jewish sects of the time. Chief among these sects were the Sadducees and the Pharisees.

The disciples came into conflict with the sect of the Sadducees, as Jesus had done during his last days at Jerusalem, in the person of the high priest and his legal advisors. Like Jesus, they are reported to have preached in the public courtyards of the temple which the Sadducean priesthood controlled. No sooner had they begun to proclaim that God had raised Jesus from the dead and appointed him as Messiah, than they were arrested and warned not to speak to anyone in his name. Luke opened his report of their arrest with these words:

> As they were speaking to the people, the priests and the captain of
> the temple and the Sadducees came upon them, annoyed because

they were teaching the people and proclaiming in Jesus the resurrection from the dead. (Acts 4:1-2)

Near the end of Acts, Luke explained this annoyance of the Sadducees over the announcement of the resurrection.

Paul stood before the council of the high priest, and noticing that there were present not only Sadducees but some Pharisees, cried out:

Brethren, I am a Pharisee, a son of Pharisees; with respect to the hope and the resurrection of the dead I am on trial. (Acts 23:6)

Immediately there was dissension between the two rival sects and the assembly was divided, for—as Luke explained—"the Sadducees say that there is no resurrection, nor angel, nor spirit; but the Pharisees acknowledge them all." So some scribes of the sect of the Pharisees took Paul's side, saying, "We find nothing wrong in this man. What if a spirit or an angel spoke to him?" In other words, on the basis of their own beliefs Pharisees could admit the possibility that the Messiah had spoken to Paul on the road to Damascus, even though they might not agree that Jesus is the Messiah. The Sadducees denied both possibilities.

However, Theophilus did not have to wait until near the end of the book of Acts for this explanation of the opposition of the Sadducees to the sect of the "Nazarenes," for Luke had already made the situation clear in his first volume. There he had reported an encounter between Jesus and "some Sadducees, those who say that there is no resurrection." In true legalistic fashion they attempted to reduce the idea to an absurdity, by relating the story of a woman who had been married successively to seven brothers: "In the resurrection, therefore, whose wife will she be?" To this riddle Jesus replied that conditions of life in the age to come are different from those of this life, and appealed to the scriptures in support of the faith that the dead of past ages are alive to God. (Luke 20:27-38)

It is significant that the scripture which Jesus cited was the account of Moses at the burning bush, for the Sadducees were bound to acknowledge its authority. Explaining the differences between the Sadducees and the Pharisees, the first-century Jewish historian, Josephus, had this to say:

> The Pharisees have delivered to the people a great many observances by succession from their fathers, which are not written in the law of Moses; and for that reason the Sadducees reject them. (*Antiquities* XIII:x:6)

But if the law itself, in the book of Exodus, called the Lord, "the God of Abraham and the God of Isaac and the God of Jacob," then these men of ancient times were thought of as still living, for "he is not God of the dead but of the living." Perhaps this argument did not convince the Sadducees, but it silenced them for the moment.

Yet the opposition of the Sadducees to Jesus and his followers was more serious than a mere difference of opinion about the life to come. The Pharisees, who also held the doctrine of the resurrection, were not attacked as the "Nazarenes" were. No doubt their position was already too secure for the priests to have risked action against them, but there are other reasons why the followers of Jesus were opposed. It was possible to tolerate the belief in a general resurrection of the dead at some future day, since the idea defied proof or disproof. It was quite another matter when the claim was made that God had actually raised up a particular dead man. Especially a man whom the Sadducean priests themselves had brought to trial before the Roman governor with the accusation:

> We found this man perverting our nation, and forbidding us to give tribute to Caesar, and saying that he himself is Christ a king. (Luke 23:2)

Thus the Sadducees appear in the gospel record, as they are known in history, not only as a religious sect, but as a political party.

While the exact origin of this party is uncertain, at the time of Jesus its adherents were largely members of the landed aristocracy and the priestly families. It is scarcely surprising that they enjoyed no popularity among the masses, since they could only maintain their position through collaboration with the Romans, the real rulers of Palestine. Although the priesthood was hereditary, the Roman procurator of Judea claimed and exercised the right to appoint the high priest and to depose him if he did not prove cooperative. This had happened to Annas, the father-in-law of Caiaphas, whose name is familiar in the gospel records.

Facts like these furnished eloquent commentary on the warning of Jesus that no man can serve two masters. No matter how sincerely some of the Sadducean priests may have desired to serve God, they were obliged to serve Ceasar also. Their obligations to the Roman government go far to explain the part they played in the tragic events which brought Jesus to the cross. It is less likely that they were able to exert pressure on Pilate to take reluctant action, than that they acted under direct orders from him when they arrested Jesus and indicted him as one who threatened the peace and security of the nation. So completely had they failed to understand his gospel of the kingdom of God that they identified his aims with those of the revolutionary Jewish nationalists who sought only to re-establish a worldly monarchy.

The quarrel of the Sadducees with the sect of the "Nazarenes" was simply a continuation of their quarrel with Jesus. They were offended that "uneducated, common men" not only defied their power, but even dared to rebuke them for having "denied the Holy and Righteous One." In disobedience to the orders of the council, these Galilean peasants had dared to reply:

> Whether it is right in the sight of God to listen to you rather than to God, you must judge; for we cannot but speak of what we have seen and heard. (Acts 4:19-20)

The right to be different, the right of private judgment in matters of conscience, was never more clearly asserted. It was as if the disciples had said: God has spoken to us. As for you priests, who in ancient times were entrusted with divine oracles, there is no evidence that God now speaks through you to the people!

When the order not to teach in the name of Jesus was repeated, it was met with further defiance: "We must obey God rather than men." (Acts 5:29) Small wonder if the council were enraged and wanted to put Peter and the other apostles to death. But, the report continued, a certain Pharisee named Gamaliel gave juster and saner advice. He reminded the council that this was not the first time in recent history that the country had been disturbed by upstarts who for a short time had a popular following, only to meet defeat at the hands of the Romans, so that their movements had come to nothing. He concluded, with reference to the followers of Jesus:

> If this plan or this undertaking is of men, it will fail; but if it is of God, you will not be able to overthrow them. You might even be found opposing God! (Acts 5:38-39)

Acting on this advice, the council repeated its warnings, made more emphatic by a beating, and let the apostles go.

One of the two popular leaders named in this short speech by Gamaliel was Judas the Galilean. He was the reputed founder of another sect among the Jews, the political party of the Zealots. The Jewish historian Josephus left a fuller account of the revolt which Judas had led against the census imposed by Quirinius, the Roman governor of Syria. The revolutionary patriot had asserted that Jews would be cowardly slaves if they submitted to taxation by Caesar. His followers, according to Josephus, agreed in other respects with the teachings of the Pharisees, but in their fanatical devotion to freedom they were willing to risk death rather than call any man lord. God was to be their only ruler and Lord. It was hardly necessary for Josephus to point out to readers in his day that "lord" was one of the divine titles claimed by several of the Roman emperors.

One of the Dead Sea Scrolls outlines preparations to be made by the "sons of light" for a last victorious war against the "sons of darkness." Consequently, a few scholars have suggested that the community of Jews that produced this document may have been a band of Zealots, or persons closely allied with that party in opposing Roman rule. But much of the language describing this "war," in which not only human but angelic warriors were to engage against "the army of Belial," seems to be intended no more literally than similar military metaphors used in expressing the eschatological hopes of early Christians. (II Thessalonians 1:5—2:12; Ephesians 6:10-17; Revelation 12:7-17; 19:11-21) Whatever else such poetic imagery may indicate, there is nothing to suggest that the writers of New Testament books which contain them intended to rally their readers to a desperate revolt against the Roman empire, even if some of them, like the author of Revelation, thought of that empire as the embodiment of Satanic evil.

While some Roman rulers were men of ability and broad tolerance, many of them showed little understanding for the moral and religious convictions of their Jewish subjects. It must have been difficult for the ordinary man to distinguish clearly between patriotism and religion, between national independence for Israel and the sovereignty of God. It may seem ironical that Jesus, who proclaimed the gospel of God's reign, should have been crucified as a political revolutionary who claimed to be "King of the Jews." But in the eyes of Romans, and even of the Sadducean council, his devotion to the kingdom of God may have seemed enough like the fanaticism of the Zealots to have justified the action of the authorities against him.

Against this background, certain details in the gospels take on added significance. In his second volume, Luke had to report Gamaliel's implied comparison between the followers of Jesus

and those of Judas, the Galilean rebel. He must have been eager
to do all that he could to correct such misconceptions of the
church's doctrine that Jesus is the Christ. Thus, near the beginning of his gospel, Luke made direct reference to the very census
taken by Quirinius against which Judas had led his revolt. In
marked contrast to such violence, the parents of Jesus had submitted without protest to the decree of Caesar Augustus, which
necessitated their journey from Nazareth to Bethlehem. So it
came about that the Christian Messiah was born in "the city of
David." Yet the place of his birth was not a royal palace, nor
even a house, but the rude shelter of a stable, for his mother "laid
him in a manger, because there was no place for them in the inn."
(Luke 2:1-7)

However, in his lists of the twelve apostles, Luke did record
the name of a man still known as "Simon the Zealot." (Luke
6:15; Acts 1:13) If the term "Zealot" was meant here in the par-
tisan political sense, it would be instructive to discover how this
man came to be a follower of Jesus. He might have joined his
company under the illusion that the aims of Jesus were similar to
those of his former associates. But in that case he must have
undergone serious disappointment when he learned the real
meaning of the message and mission of Jesus. It seems more
likely that Simon abandoned the Zealot cause, when he came to
realize from Jesus the error of those men of violence who tried to
take the kingdom of heaven by force. (Matthew 11:12)

Politically the Sadducees and the Zealots stood at opposite
poles in their attitude toward the Roman government, while a
somewhat neutral ground was taken by the sects of the Pharisees
and of the Essenes. The Essenes, who are not even mentioned
in the New Testament, were dominated by a lofty ideal, the ideal
of holiness. Yet they seem to have supposed that such an ideal
could be attained only in isolation from the world. Disillusioned
by conditions within their nation, they even abandoned the society of their fellow Jews to inhabit the desolate region near the

western shore of the Dead Sea, where the Roman writer, Pliny the elder, described them as living with only palm trees for companions.

Josephus praised their ascetic virtues and their hospitality toward traveling members of their sect. Yet marriage and family life, held in highest honor in the Hebrew scriptures, were given up by most, if not all, Essenes. To emphasize their purity, they practiced daily ritual ablutions and affected white garments. It is preposterous to suggest, as some have done, that Jesus and his followers could be "explained" by the theory that he was at one time associated with the Essenes. They would have been quite as quick as any Pharisean scribe to criticize him for eating with "sinners." Such criticism shows that there was nothing in his life suggesting ascetic withdrawal from the world. When the Pharisees and the disciples of John were observing some extra fast, Jesus defended his own followers in their failure to abstain from eating. His presence made every meal like a wedding feast. (Mark 2:18-22) He even admitted that some people said of him, "Behold, a glutton and a drunkard, a friend of tax collectors and sinners!" (Matthew 11:19) Granted that the accusation of overindulgence was a gross slander, one cannot imagine anyone calling an Essene "a friend of sinners," even in jest.

New light is being sought regarding such ascetic sects among the Jews, by a study of the Dead Sea Scrolls, especially the *Manual of Discipline*. That there were some similarities of thought and practice between the community that produced these documents and that of the early church is scarcely surprising. Both were heirs to the common cultural and religious heritage of Judaism. But the differences between the two groups are of particular importance for any clear understanding of the distinctive character of each. The people of the Scrolls, whom many scholars regard as identical with the Essenes, followed a very strict code of rules, separating themselves from all men of error by dwelling in the wilderness. Their community overlooking the shores of the Dead Sea was controlled by a committee of priests, in whom was invested all authority over judicial and financial affairs. At meetings they were careful to observe a rigid order of hierarchical precedence. The priests were seated first, then the elders, and after them the rest of the company according to rank. At meals of the community, the priest first extended his hand over the bread and the wine to pronounce a blessing. This practice may help to link these people with the Essenes, since Josephus reported that the latter regarded it unlawful for any of their members to eat until grace had been said by a priest.

How different all this was from the practice of the first disciples of Jesus is plain from the New Testament. Their teacher had refused to assign to any of them places of special privilege, warning that there must be no positions of rank among them. When he pointed out that such distinctions were characteristic of the Gentiles, this was the equivalent of calling it "heathen" behavior. (Mark 10:35-45) Although not of priestly descent, Jesus said the blessings at their common meals. Yet even then, he reminded his disciples that he was among them as a servant, in pointed rebuke of their ambitious rivalry for high position. (Mark 6:41; 8:6; 14:22; Luke 22:14-27)

It is noteworthy that the only priests mentioned in the gospels belonged to the Sadducean hierarchy, which collaborated with the Roman governor in condemning Jesus to death—unless Zechariah, the father of John the baptizer, is to be regarded as an exception. (Luke 1:5) Since it is possible to find other similarities between John and the Scroll people, his priestly ancestry may be of significance, but it tells us nothing of importance about primitive Christianity. Nor does Luke's statement in his second volume, that "many of the priests were obedient to the faith." (Acts 6:7) Since the discovery of the Scrolls, an abnormal amount of attention has been given to this statement. Yet it is the last that we ever hear of these priests, whoever they were, and no evidence is forthcoming to demonstrate that they continued to function as priests if and when they actually joined the community of the disciples.

As we have already observed, part of his preparation for his mission was a brief period spent by Jesus in the wilderness, popularly known as "the temptation." After a few days of wrestling with problems confronting him on his course, he returned to Galilee. Later, when the twelve messengers he had sent on a preaching tour returned to report their activities, he invited them to go into an uninhabited part of the country in order to obtain some rest. (Mark 6:30-32) Surely such a temporary retreat for physical relaxation bears no resemblance to the permanent withdrawal from society, which was the central feature in the discipline of the Scroll people. Neither during the lifetime of Jesus, nor in the period following his resurrection, does the New Testament record any comparable attempt on the part of his followers to settle in the wilderness. Nor does it reveal any drastic efforts to separate themselves from possible defilement by association with other people less pious or holy. This motive of separation, which accounts for the establishment of the Scroll community, the ruins of whose buildings are still to be seen on the rim of the *Wadi Qumran,* is diametrically opposed to the purpose of Jesus as we know it from the gospels.

With regard to one of the most fundamental observances of Judaism, the sabbath day, Jesus and his disciples stood in striking contrast to the practices of the community by the Dead Sea, as well as the Essenes, if these two are not identical. The *Manual of Discipline* lays down rules for keeping the holy day, which are even stricter than those of the Pharisees, who often accused Jesus or his disciples of violations. (Mark 2:23-3:6; Luke 13:10-17; 14:1-6) The New Testament furnishes no conclusive evidence how further differences with Jewish sabbath practice arose. Eventually early Christianity abandoned the observance of the seventh day completely. One instance is recorded of an assembly for worship on the first day of the week. (Acts 20:7) It is generally believed that this day was chosen because, as the gospels report, it was the day on which Jesus rose from the dead. (Mark 16:2; John 20:1) Nevertheless, Paul's letters furnish evidence of a time in the primitive church when there was no common agreement on such matters. Some regarded "one day better than another," while others regarded all days alike. (Romans 14:5) Thus one might go on, if it were necessary, to demonstrate how many significant differences distinguished the followers of Jesus from the sect that produced the Scrolls, as well as from other groupings among the Jews, even though the beliefs which they held in common were not altogether insignificant.

The controversies between Jesus and the Pharisees are thoroughly familiar to every reader of the gospels. Differences over sabbath observance, fasting, eating with "sinners," or without ceremonial ablutions, as well as over other traditions, are all mentioned in the earliest accounts. (Mark 2:15-3:6; 7:1-13) Events seem to have taken a new turn after the movement of his followers began to spread beyond the borders of Palestine, and to draw converts from among the Gentiles. Doubtless some adherents of the Pharisean party, who looked forward to the general resurrection of the dead, were attracted to the gospel proclamation that this hope had already begun to be realized in the resurrection of Jesus himself. But Luke also mentions that "some believers who belonged to the party of the Pharisees" rose up in the congregation at Jerusalem to urge that it was necessary for Gentile converts to accept circumcision and to keep the law of Moses. (Acts 15:5) If the record in the Acts is correct, none of the leaders of the new sect agreed to this demand, although a more conservative group, headed by James, laid down certain requirements which Gentile converts must observe if they were to be admitted to table fellowship with Jewish believers. (Acts 15:23-29) From Paul's letter to the churches in Galatia, it is evident that this position was taken by James, the brother of the Lord, and that pressure from the group which he led caused

Peter, and even Barnabas—Paul's earliest associate in the mission among the Gentiles—to separate themselves, at least temporarily, from the common meals at which Gentile converts were present. (Galatians 1:18-2:14)

But by this time the new sect was beginning to acquire a new name, one which was to continue in use long after the meaning of the term *Nazoree*, or *Nazarene*, was lost in obscurity. It was in Antioch, in Syria, the headquarters of the Gentile mission, that the disciples were first called *Christians*. Appropriate as this name may have appeared, it was evidently one given to the movement by outsiders, and slow in gaining acceptance among the disciples themselves, for it is used only three times in the entire New Testament. (Acts 11:26; 26:28; I Peter 4:16) It was by this name, as we have seen, that the followers of Jesus were first mentioned in Roman histories like that of Tacitus.

Since the Greek term *Christ* was the equivalent of the Hebrew *Messiah*, the description of the disciples as Christians served to designate them as followers of the Anointed One. Yet there were many other Jews who looked forward to the coming of the Lord's Anointed some day. What distinguished these Christians was their faith that the Messiah had already come, or that he had at least been revealed, in the person of Jesus the crucified.

As his followers continued his mission, they did not simply repeat his own message that men should repent because God's reign was at hand. They gave that message a fresh urgency and a different emphasis:

> Repent, and be baptized every one of you in the name of Jesus Christ for the forgiveness of your sins; and you shall receive the gift of the Holy Spirit. (Acts 2:38)

The preachers of this message were bold in their assertion of their right to differ from other Jews, claiming that their own testimony to the messiahship of Jesus was supported by the witness of "the Holy Spirit whom God has given to those who obey him." (Acts 5:32) It remained for them to demonstrate that the liberty which they were denied by the official leaders of Judaism could be maintained in their own community by the manifestation of unity through diversity rather than enforced uniformity. Such was the unity which the apostle Paul was to proclaim:

> For by one Spirit we were all baptized into one body—Jews or Greeks, slaves or free—and were all made to drink of one Spirit. (I Corinthians 12:13)

By that time what had begun as a sect of the Jews had become in truth the church of the living God, the fellowship of the Spirit.

CHAPTER THREE

THE FELLOWSHIP
OF THE SPIRIT

ALTHOUGH the cross loomed high on the horizon between the old community of Israel and the growing body of Jews and Gentiles who put their faith in Jesus Christ, the line of demarcation which separated them was not at first clearly defined. Christian faith met its severest test, its most difficult obstacle, in the fact that Jesus had been sentenced to die by crucifixion. The preaching of "Christ crucified" was, as Paul well knew, a stumbling-block to Jews and folly to Gentiles. (I Corinthians 1:23)

A stumbling-block! From Paul's own Greek word for it we get our word "scandal"—something which offends the mind and moral sense of men—a disgrace to religion. No wonder many Jews felt this way about the claim that the man whom Pilate had hanged on the gallows was their anointed king, God's Messiah. Their legal experts must have been quick to retort that the law had declared: ". . . a hanged man is accursed by God." (Deuteronomy 21:23)

None knew this better than Paul himself, for he had been a bitter persecutor of the sect of the Nazarenes. Years after his conversion to faith in Jesus, he still remembered and repeated those awful words which had once made the story of the cross as offensive to him as it continued to be to so many of his fellow Jews. Yet looking back at the death of Christ in the new light of his resurrection, Paul could no longer speak of the law's curse as God's curse. On the contrary, he affirmed that by his death Christ has redeemed men from that curse, that the blessing which God promised to Abraham might come upon people of all nations. The great fulfillment of that promise was the gift of the Spirit which men receive through faith in Christ. (Galatians 3:6-14) Thus it was manifestly God's purpose to unite both Jews and Gentiles in a single community established upon the confession of Jesus Christ as its chief cornerstone.

Stumbling-block and Cornerstone

The metaphor of a stumbling-block was one that Paul found in the Hebrew scriptures. Centuries earlier, Isaiah had compared God himself to such a great rock. To those who trusted him, God would become a "sanctuary," a strong place of refuge and security. But to the faithless, he would be "a stone of offense, a rock of stumbling." (Isaiah 8:13-15) Yet further on in the same book, the prophet had represented God as saying:

> Behold, I am laying in Zion for a foundation, a stone, a tested stone, a precious cornerstone, of a sure foundation: 'He who believes will not be in haste.' (Isaiah 28:16)

In such prophetic insights as these Paul found a key to the paradox that Jesus is both the crucified and the Christ, for the same rock over which some men trip and fall, may become a firm foundation for others. Quoting from memory, as people familiar with the Bible often do, not altogether accurately, Paul wove these two verses from Isaiah together when he wrote to the church at Rome:

> Behold, I am laying in Zion a stone that will make men stumble, a rock that will make them fall; and he who believes in him will not be put to shame. (Romans 9:33)

There was no doubt in Paul's mind that this rock was Christ.

The same conviction is central to Paul's warning to the church at Corinth, in which he compared the Christian community to a great building which must be erected to withstand severe and critical testing:

> No other foundation can any one lay than that which is laid, which is Jesus Christ. (I Corinthians 3:11)

Since Paul likened himself to a skilled master builder who laid this foundation, it is clear that he referred to his work as an apostle in proclaiming the gospel that Jesus is the Christ, the fundamental fact on which "God's building" rests. Whether by Paul himself, or—as some scholars contend—by some one very familiar with his teachings, this is the real significance of the statement that Christians are "built upon the foundation of the apostles and prophets, Christ Jesus himself being the chief cornerstone." (Ephesians 2:20) The apostles' and prophets' foundation is the one which they laid by their testimony to Jesus as Messiah. Thus they were "fellow workmen for God."

Nor are such thoughts peculiar to Paul's letters. Mark, who according to an early tradition served as the interpreter of the apostle Peter, recorded in his gospel that Jesus himself had quoted another scriptural reference to a cornerstone, referring it to himself:

> The very stone which the builders rejected has become the head of the corner; this is the Lord's doing, and it is marvelous in our eyes. (Mark 12:10-11; Psalm 118:22-23)

Since Jesus had been repudiated by the high priest and council at Jerusalem, the official "architects" of Judaism, such a proof text became a great favorite among his disciples. The historian Luke described Peter as using this text in a defense of the new faith before the same Jewish leaders who had drawn up the indictment which brought Jesus to his death on the cross. (Acts 4:5-12)

Probably nowhere in the New Testament was the affirmation that Jesus Christ is the "rock" of Isaiah 8:14-15, as well as the "cornerstone" of Isaiah 28:16 and Psalm 118:22, given fuller expression than in the first letter of Peter. The writer drew a vivid word picture of believers as "living stones" built into a spiritual "house," of which Christ is the chosen cornerstone. If he mixed his metaphors, by going on to call believers "a holy priesthood," that may well be due to the conviction that the Jewish hierarchy had shown themselves unfit to lead the worship of a "holy nation" by their rejection of the Messiah. To them Jesus Christ had been "a rock to make men fall," a stumbling block and cause of offense. (I Peter 2:4-9) Although some modern scholars question the authenticity of the tradition regarding this letter, from fairly early times it was believed to have been sent by the apostle Peter from Rome, symbolically referred to as "Babylon." (I Peter 5:13)

A Parable About God's House

The conviction that Christ himself is the rock upon which the church is built was still firmly held among Christians at Rome during the first half of the second century when a teacher named Hermas published a book called *The Shepherd*, or *Pastor*. This book was so highly regarded that several church writers of the next century referred to it as scripture. In fact an important Greek manuscript of the fourth or fifth century, Codex Sinaiticus, included the text of *The Shepherd* of Hermas at the end of the New Testament. One list of New Testament books, compiled toward the end of the second century, known as the Muratorian fragment, had this to say about it:

Hermas composed the *Shepherd* very recently in our times in the city of Rome, while his brother Pius the bishop was sitting on the cathedra of the church in the city of Rome, and therefore it ought to be read, although it cannot be published to the people in church, either among the prophets which are complete in number, or among the apostles, to the end of time.

Yet, although Hermas was neither a prophet nor an apostle, his book is not without value for us. Most scholars would date its actual composition earlier than A.D. 140-155, the supposed time of the episcopate of Pius, pointing out that Hermas mentions his association with Clement, who is said to have presided over the Roman congregation around A.D. 95. The text of *The Shepherd* is readily available in English translation for anyone interested in reading it, in the collection of early Christian documents known as *The Apostolic Fathers*. It is divided into three parts: the Visions, the Commandments, and the Parables.

In his ninth parable, Hermas described a symbolic tower which he had seen being built upon a great white rock. The Greek word for "rock" in this parable, just as in Romans 9:33 and I Peter 2:8, is *petra*. But Hermas seems to have patterned the first part of his story directly on the one which Jesus had told about the house built upon the rock, where the same word *petra* is used in the Greek text of the gospels. (Matthew 7:24-25; Luke 6:48) Hermas not only referred to the tower as God's "house," but emphasized that it was not built on the ground (like the house of the foolish man), but upon the rock. It is impossible to observe here all the elaborate and often fanciful details with which Hermas embellished his picture of this building. For example, the statement that the stones placed in the foundation upon the rock must first go down into the water and come up from it obviously refers to the requirement of baptism. And when Hermas says that there was a pause in the work of construction because the Lord was coming to test the building, he may have had in mind Paul's warning about the day of testing. (I Corinthians 3:12-15)

However, the detail which excited the keenest interest for

Hermas is the one of principal importance for us. After saying that the rock was higher than the mountains and perfectly square, so that it could contain the whole world, he added that this rock was an ancient one. Yet a gate had recently been hewn out of this rock, so that every one entering the tower must pass through this new gate. When at last the meaning of this vision was revealed to him, Hermas explained the allegorical significance of these points to his readers. The tower is the church, the *ekklesia,* and the rock, or *petra,* upon which it is built is the Son of God. The paradox between the antiquity of the rock and the newly cut gate is likewise symbolic. For although the Son of God is older than his creation, he was manifested in the last days, in order that those who are to be saved may enter into the kingdom of heaven. Thus Christ is both the cornerstone of the church and the door through which believers find entrance into God's eternal reign.

Upon This Rock

This long succession of testimony, preserved in no less than four documents believed to have been connected with the early church at Rome, is certainly instructive. Careful attention to it is indispensable for a proper understanding of a now famous saying attributed to Jesus, which has become a storm center of ecclesiastical controversy. In approaching this saying, it is important to notice the setting given to it in the Gospel according to Matthew. In the earliest written record of his ministry, when Jesus asked his disciples, "Who do you say that I am?" Peter answered, "You are the Christ." At once Jesus commanded them to tell no one about it. (Mark 8:27-30) Luke followed Mark's account very closely, except that he worded Peter's reply somewhat more biblically, "The Christ of God," that is, God's Anointed. (Luke 9:20)

The Gospel according to Matthew is unique in the addition of certain new and striking details to this story. When Peter asserted, "You are the Christ, the Son of the living God," Jesus is reported to have answered him:

> Blessed are you, Simon Bar-Jona! For flesh and blood has not revealed this to you, but my Father who is in heaven. And I tell you, you are Peter, and on this rock I will build my church, and the powers of death shall not prevail against it. I will give you the keys of the kingdom of heaven, and whatever you bind on earth shall be bound in heaven, and whatever you loose on earth shall be loosed in heaven. (Matthew 16:17-19)

Few readers of the Bible need to be told that this is the chief text of scripture on which the church of Rome now bases its claim to universal authority. Probably every visitor to the modern Vatican State has stood beneath the imposing dome of Saint Peter's basilica, looking up at this very text in Latin, emblazoned around the rotunda in gilt letters seven feet high: *Tu es Petrus, et super hanc petram aedificabo ecclesiam meam. . . .* What is the real significance of these words?

Whoever reads and attempts to interpret this saying needs to be aware of a serious and difficult problem, still being debated among biblical scholars, whether Jesus ever actually spoke these words. No Roman Catholic scholar would be permitted to express uncertainty on this question, which Protestant scholars can and do discuss freely and frankly. As a result of this free enquiry, there is naturally difference of opinion among non-Roman students of the gospels. Some would defend the authenticity of the tradition on the ground that the language of the saying appears to be characteristically Jewish, as well as that Peter often stood out prominently among the disciples. Yet the Acts indicate that it was not he, but James the brother of the Lord, who actually exercised the position of leadership in the council of "the apostles and the elders," even though Peter was present. (Acts 15:6-7; 13-21) Paul, too, mentioned James before Peter (Cephas) and John, a fact which hardly suggests that Peter was the most prominent among these "pillars." (Galatians 2:9)

Other scholars, who question whether Jesus actually spoke these words to Peter, point out that if Jesus had informed the disciples that it was his intention to found a new church, they would hardly have continued to attend services in the Jewish synagogues or in the temple at Jerusalem, as the Acts show them to have done for many years after his death and resurrection. They also point out that the word *church* occurs only one other time in any saying attributed to Jesus, where it probably refers to the local congregation of a Jewish synagogue. (Matthew 18:17)

Even scholars who accept the saying as genuine disagree over its proper place in the gospel tradition. Some think that it was misplaced by the evangelist, having originally been part of a warning given to Peter just before the arrest of Jesus, which in turn led to Peter's denial of his Master:

> Simon, Simon, behold, Satan demanded to have you, that he might sift you like wheat, but I have prayed for you that your faith may not fail; and when you have turned again, strengthen your brethren. (Luke 22:31-32)

According to this view, when Peter's faith recovered from the scandal of the cross, he could become a "rock" of strength for the faith of others. Still other scholars point out that the words "the powers of death . . ." or, more literally, "the gates of Hades shall not prevail," may have been part of a conversation that took place when Christ first appeared to Peter after his resurrection. (Luke 24:34; John 21:15-18; I Corinthians 15:5) All such attempts to find a more appropriate setting for these words stem from a common recognition that the eulogy to Peter is strikingly out of harmony with its present context.

This incongruity is evident from the fact that all the evangelists who report Peter's confession agree that it became the occasion of a sharp conflict of opinion with his Master about the true mission of the Messiah. It is clear from these accounts that when Peter first called Jesus "the Christ," he meant something so foreign to the intention of his Master that he brought upon himself a stinging rebuke: "Get behind me, Satan! You are a hindrance to me; for you are not on the side of God, but of men." (Matthew 16:23) The Greek word translated "hindrance" here is the same as "stumbling-block." That was as much of a rock as Peter could be called, when he tried to tempt Jesus from the way of the cross, to follow the way of the sword! In fact, it was only by way of the cross and the resurrection of Jesus that Peter and the rest of the disciples came to understand that Christ was not the long-expected warrior king of Jewish nationalistic hopes, but that his saving mission was for all men everywhere.

Whatever the origin of the words "upon this rock," the problem of basic concern is to determine their meaning. The disciple to whom they are said to have been addressed was given the Greek name *Petros,* while the word for "rock" is the feminine noun *petra.* Defenders of the saying point out that in Aramaic the word for "rock" would be the same as the name *Keipha,* or "Cephas," by which this disciple was also known. (John 1:42; Galatians 1:18—2:14) But if, by giving him this name, Jesus had intended to designate Peter as the rock on which the future church would be built, why did Mark—"the interpreter of Peter" —omit any record of the words? Why did Peter himself, or whoever it was that wrote an epistle in his name, likewise fail to mention them in connection with the building of the spiritual house? Why did this writer, like Paul, and long afterward Hermas, speak of Christ alone as the "rock" or *petra,* the cornerstone on which the church is built? These are important questions.

Perhaps a reasonable answer can be found to such questions, by considering again the nature of the warning issued to the

Corinthian church when factions began to divide the congregation. Some members said, "I belong to Paul"; others, "I belong
to Apollos"; still others said, "I belong to Cephas." Refusing to
have any sect calling itself after his name, the great apostle to the
Gentiles reminded his readers that none of them had been baptized in his name. They had been baptized in the name of
Christ, who was crucified for them. (I Corinthians 1:10-13)
Then he went on to ask, "What is Apollos? What is Paul?" These
human agents of the gospel message, he insisted, were simply
"servants" through whom men were brought to faith in Christ.
"We are fellow workmen for God. . . . I laid a foundation, and
another man is building upon it. . . . For no other foundation
can anyone lay than that which is laid, which is Jesus Christ."
(I Corinthians 3:5-11)

If the question were asked, "What is Peter?" the answer would
certainly have been the same. He, too, was a servant of God
through whom men were brought to faith in Jesus Christ. Perhaps it was true, as the earliest gospel record said, that Peter
was the first disciple to call Jesus the Messiah. Yet it must not
be overlooked that another ancient tradition stated that this recognition was first made by Andrew, Peter's less famous brother,
who introduced him to Jesus. Seeking out his brother Simon,
he said, "We have found the Messiah." (John 1:41) From this
striking variation in the New Testament records, we may conclude that the thing which really mattered was not the name
of the particular spokesman who voiced this faith. All that mattered was the faith itself.

Without the conviction that Jesus, though rejected and crucified by men, is the Christ, the Son of God, Andrew and Peter
and the rest of their companions might have remained pious
Jews, still hoping for the coming of God's Anointed. Indeed,
without that faith, what we call the Christian church would
never have been built. It is that faith which all Christians, by
whatever other name they may be called, still share. Only where

that faith is kept central can the church stand united. One of the great hymns of Christian faith reaffirms the fundamental conviction of the earliest believers: "The church's one foundation is Jesus Christ her Lord." To build on any other foundation would be to build on sand.

The Easter Faith

In a very real sense the story of the church in the New Testament takes its beginning from the event which marks the climax of all the gospel narratives, the revelation that Jesus who was crucified has risen. Yet the earliest sources of our information concerning the events which shaped the Christian faith and gave to the Christian community its distinctive character are neither the gospels, nor their sequel, the Acts of the Apostles, but the letters of Paul, written between A.D. 50 and 63. This is rather significant because Paul's own faith in Jesus Christ began with the events which followed the crucifixion, not with any of those which had preceded it. For Paul, faith in Jesus had never been associated with those political misconceptions of his messiahship which had been dashed to disappointment by his execution as "King of the Jews." The only allusion to this dynastic conception of the Messiah in any of Paul's letters shows how completely it was transcended by another. For although Christ was "descended from David according to the flesh," the heart of the gospel is that he was "designated Son of God with power according to the Spirit of holiness by his resurrection from the dead." (Romans 1:3-4) Thus Paul could go on to affirm, "If you confess with your lips that Jesus is Lord, and believe in your heart that God raised him from the dead, you will be saved." (Romans 10:9)

For Paul, everything hinged on this event, to which he could testify because he had seen the risen Lord. That had been the turning point in Paul's life, which had converted him from a persecutor of the church to an apostle of Jesus Christ. He linked his own personal testimony with that of others before him, in a letter he wrote to a Christian congregation already disturbed by doubts about the reality of the resurrection:

> I delivered to you as of first importance what I also received, that Christ died for our sins in accordance with the scriptures, that he was buried, that he was raised on the third day in accordance with the scriptures, and that he appeared to Cephas, then to the twelve. Then he appeared to more than five hundred brethren at one time, most of whom are still alive, though some have fallen asleep. Then he appeared to James, then to all the apostles. Last of all, as to one untimely born, he appeared also to me. (I Corinthians 15:3-8)

At this early date, what counted was the witness borne by the many individuals whose lives had been so deeply affected by the presence of the living Christ.

Neither in this, nor in any other letter, did Paul attempt to describe the appearance of the risen Lord. In answer to members of the Corinthian church who were saying, "There is no resurrection of the dead," he insisted that he and the rest of the apostles had not borne false witness in their preaching of the gospel. If he was familiar with a report about the discovery of the empty tomb, first published in Mark's gospel, he made no mention of it. Such a report by itself would have proved nothing, since opponents among the Jews soon countered it with the charge that the disciples had stolen away the body of Jesus during the night. (Matthew 28:13) One of the later evangelists described the risen Jesus as having a body of flesh and bones still nourished by eating food. (Luke 24:36-43) At least, he was recognized, according to the fourth gospel, by the print of the nails in his hands. Nevertheless, the story of doubting Thomas, who had demanded such evidence, concluded with a gentle rebuke: "Blessed are those who have not seen and yet believe." (John 20:24-29)

It is clear that Paul thought of the resurrection as involving a great transformation from a physical body, to what he called a "spiritual body." (I Corinthians 15:42-50) If the word "spiritual" has acquired in modern thought an element of vagueness, or even of unreality, we can be sure that this was far from Paul's intention when he used this term. Since he spoke of the spiritual body as "imperishable," it is obvious that he meant by it something more permanently real than a physical body which is "perishable" through the decay that follows death. While Paul was speaking specifically about the future resurrection of believers, all that he said about this was patterned on what he believed to be true of Christ himself. For Paul believed that when Christ comes, he will "change our lowly body to be like his glorious body." (Philippians 3:21) For most devout believers it was enough to have this assurance that when Christ appears, we shall be like him. (I John 3:2)

It is important to bear in mind that in this earliest period of Christian faith the resurrection of Christ was regarded as an eschatological event. It marked the beginning of the Messiah's triumph over all opposition to God's final and complete reign. As the "first fruits," it furnished the assurance of the ultimate gathering of the full harvest when all who are in Christ will be made alive. (I Corinthians 15:20-28; I Thessalonians 4:13-17) More than this, it gave believers confidence to endure whatever trials might come upon them before that glorious end, for it meant that the living Christ would always be in their midst as they gathered together in his name until the close of this age. (Matthew 18:20; 28:20) As the life-giving Spirit, dwelling within believers, Christ gave them power to live a new life here and now, as well as the hope of glory still to come. (I Corinthians 15:45; Romans 8:9-11; Galatians 2:20; Colossians 1:27)

The Meaning of Pentecost

When Luke the evangelist published the sequel to his gospel, known as the Acts of the Apostles, he tried to make clear to his readers that there was a close connection between two events which were understood to have eschatological significance: the resurrection of Jesus, and the fresh outpouring of the Holy Spirit which emboldened the disciples to proclaim him as the Christ. By the time that Luke wrote these two books, the generation of the original "eyewitnesses," as he called them, belonged to the past. (Luke 1:2) Looked at from the perspective gained through the church's steady growth and its advance across the Roman world, it was natural that the actual occurrences should have taken on new and wider meanings, so that the description of them appears highly symbolic.

The risen Lord had charged his disciples to remain at Jerusalem, there to await the promise of the Father which they had heard from him. "For John baptized with water, but before many days you shall be baptized with the Holy Spirit." Since this promised baptism with the Holy Spirit had been so closely bound up with the coming of a day of judgment and the establishment of God's reign, the old national hopes began to revive in their minds. So they had asked him, "Lord, will you at this time restore the kingdom to Israel?" But he had answered in words that revealed his universal mission to bring about the redemption of all mankind:

> It is not for you to know times or seasons which the Father has fixed by his own authority. But you shall receive power when the Holy Spirit has come upon you; and you shall be my witnesses in Jerusalem and in all Judea and Samaria and to the end of the earth. (Acts 1:7-8)

So they continued to gather in the upper room where they were staying, and with one accord devoted themselves to prayer.

Luke estimated that the company of the brethren at this time was about a hundred and twenty. This number, like that of the twelve apostles, probably had symbolic significance. It had been said that these twelve men were to sit on thrones in Christ's kingdom, judging the twelve tribes of Israel. (Luke 22:28-30) Since ten male Jews could constitute a new synagogue, one hundred and twenty would be sufficient to provide a congregation for each of the twelve tribes, each under the leadership of an apostle. Thus this number may have been mentioned to indicate that the church in the New Testament represented a reconstitution of the congregation of Israel in the Old Testament.

So important was the symbolic number "twelve," that Luke next went on to relate how selection was made of a qualified witness to the resurrection, to take the place in the ministry of the apostles from which Judas had fallen by his betrayal of the Lord. The brethren put forward two men, and after they had prayed the Lord to show which one he had chosen, they cast lots. When the lot fell on Matthias, he was enrolled with the eleven apostles. (Acts 1:15-26) It is clear that this was not regarded as an "election," but rather as a commission from Christ himself. Consequently Matthias could have said of himself as truly as Paul was to say later: "an apostle—not from men, nor through man, but through Jesus Christ and God the Father, who raised him from the dead." (Galatians 1:1)

It was the treachery of Judas, not the fact that he was dead, which necessitated his replacement among the twelve. Later, when Herod killed James the brother of John and another of the apostles, nothing similar is reported to have taken place. (Acts 12:1-2) Since it was expected that when the messianic kingdom was established, there would be a resurrection of the dead, including, of course, the martyrs, James could then take the place assigned him by the Lord. Meanwhile, it was the mission of the apostles to bear witness to the resurrection of Jesus Christ. This gives us the necessary key for understanding the nature of the "apostolic" church, in the New Testament sense of that term. It is a witnessing church.

When the day of Pentecost came, the brethren were all together in one place. The promise for which Jesus had bidden them wait was fulfilled:

> And they were all filled with the Holy Spirit and began to speak in other tongues, as the Spirit gave them utterance. (Acts 2:4)

At once a large crowd gathered, composed of Jews and other devout persons who had come to Jerusalem from all parts of the world to celebrate the feast. Originally, this had been a harvest festival, observed seven weeks after the feast of unleavened bread and connected with the Passover. Eventually the feast of Pentecost became a commemoration of the giving of the law on Mount Sinai. However, Christians had come to draw a pointed contrast between the old covenant written in the law of Moses and the new covenant given in the Spirit. (II Corinthians 3:4-18) Thus it was significant that the Holy Spirit had been poured out on the disciples on the very day dedicated to the old Mosaic covenant. This too seemed to symbolize the fact that the Christian church was commissioned by God to carry on the mission of Israel, as a light to all the nations.

When the crowd had assembled, Peter began to explain what had happened, reminding them of words spoken by the prophet Joel concerning the last days:

> I will pour out my spirit on all flesh; your sons and your daughters shall prophesy, your old men shall dream dreams, and your young men shall see visions. Even upon the menservants and maidservants in those days, I will pour out my spirit. (Joel 2:28-29)

The complete relevance of this quotation was seen in its literal fulfillment, since Luke reported the presence of both men and women among the disciples who were gathered together in the upper room, praying and waiting for the promise. The popular belief among the Jews, that prophecy had ceased after the days of Malachi, had already occasioned astonishment at the teaching of Jesus, who spoke with the authority of divine inspiration. It was recalled that John the baptizer had said that, while he baptized people with water, a mightier one would come to baptize them with the Holy Spirit. (Mark 1:7-8; Acts 1:5) The gospel writers all understood this "mightier one" to mean Jesus, on whom the Spirit had descended like a dove from heaven. Now these hopes were fulfilled as the Spirit came upon the whole company of the disciples, bringing with it a great revival of prophecy.

Still quoting his text from Joel: "Whoever calls on the name of the Lord shall be saved," Peter went on to declare that God had freed Jesus from the bonds of death, to make him both Lord and Messiah. Moved by his inspired preaching, the people asked, "What shall we do?" and received this answer:

> Repent, and be baptized every one of you in the name of Jesus Christ for the forgiveness of your sins; and you shall receive the gift of the Holy Spirit. (Acts 2:38)

So those who accepted Peter's testimony were baptized, and a great company was added to the disciples on that day. To sum up all that this decisive step meant to those who responded to the preaching of the gospel, Luke added:

> And they devoted themselves to the apostles' teaching and fellowship, to the breaking of bread and the prayers. (Acts 2:42)

The Greek word translated "fellowship" in the familiar English versions of this verse has a variety of meanings which we need to explore further if we are to understand the beginnings of the Christian church.

In the Latin version of the New Testament called the Vulgate, which is one of the oldest surviving translations from the Greek, the word used in this verse is *communicatio,* which means "shar-

ing." This fits well with "the breaking of bread." But in a number of other places (I Corinthians 1:9; Galatians 2:9; Philippians
2:1) the same Greek word was translated by the Latin *societas*,
from which we get our word "society." Bearing both these
meanings in mind, we may come to a clearer understanding of
this record in the Acts.

By repentance, outwardly signified by baptism, and by the
gift of the Holy Spirit as the assurance of God's forgiveness of
their sins, the earliest converts to faith in Jesus Christ were incorporated into a new community, without apparently severing their
lifelong association with the congregation of Israel, since Luke
reported that they also attended the temple together. (Acts
2:46) They not only shared a common allegiance to Jesus as
Messiah and Lord, which was nurtured by the teaching of the
apostles, but they also continued to come together, to share a
common meal, and to unite in common prayer. All this was an
integral part of the lasting significance of the event of Pentecost
in the memories of those who furnished Luke the information
on which he later based his record in the Acts.

In popular thought Pentecost has become known as "the
birthday of the church." Appropriate as this description may
now seem to us, Luke himself did not use the word *ekklesia*
("church") in reporting this event, probably because his inform-
ants had not used it either. At first, the company of disciples,
although still active members of the old Jewish church, discovered that they were bound to one another by even deeper ties
through the work of the Holy Spirit in their midst. Paul was to
describe this as "the fellowship of the Holy Spirit," or "participation in the Spirit." (II Corinthians 13:14; Philippians 2:1)
In this way they became a unique community with a special
mission within the larger commonwealth of Israel, which they
sought to bring to repentance and faith in Jesus Christ. Because
this profound sense of fellowship among those earliest believers
was created by the Spirit of Christ, it can rightly be called a

"spiritual unity." Certainly, any one who is aware of the divine power and reality attached to the word "Spirit" throughout the Bible, but particularly in the New Testament, must realize that there was nothing vague or indefinite about this unity and fellowship. It embraced and permeated the entire life of every believer.

For the earliest disciples this unity of the Spirit involved all that they remembered and believed concerning Jesus Christ, and the mission which he had called them to carry forward into the world. It also included even the most ordinary needs of their common life together. Luke went so far as to report:

> And all who believed were together and had all things in common; and they sold their possessions and goods and distributed them to all, as any had need. (Acts 2:44-45)

So strong was the conviction that such voluntary sharing of whatever one had for the relief of the needy was an essential part of Christian fellowship that Luke was able to illustrate it by specific examples. What is important here is not the details of these stories, but the fact that such action was taken in the growing community of the disciples. (Acts 4:32—5:11)

Fellowship in Action

Long before Luke undertook to write his history of the church's beginnings, Paul had helped to give the Greek term translated "fellowship" such wide and deep significance that he strained the bounds of ordinary language. Naturally, he often used this word in its most literal sense with reference to the actual sharing of material goods for the relief of the poor. In these cases, the most recent revision of the English Bible translates the word as "contribution." (Romans 15:26; II Corinthians 8:4; 9:13) This helps us to understand what he meant when he thanked the Philippian congregation "for your partnership in the gospel from the first day until now." (Philippians 1:5) An earlier English revision translated this, "for your fellowship in the furtherance of the gospel." From the letter that follows these words we learn more of the gratitude which Paul felt toward the Christians at Philippi, not only for a material gift either of money or provisions, but also for sending a member of their congregation to assist him while in prison. In this way they had several times proved themselves his "partners," aiding him in the work of preaching the gospel in other places. (Philippians 2:25-30; 4:10-18)

In early Christian experience, fellowship was never just a matter of amiable sentiment, but always a bond of brotherhood in Christ. It had to be demonstrated in practical service for the good of the whole community. Yet this community was not ingrown upon itself, and the best possession that believers had to communicate to those outside was the faith that made them one in Christ. Thus Paul could write in another letter: "I pray that the sharing of your faith may promote the knowledge of all the good that is ours in Christ." (Philemon 6) But Paul also knew that sharing the mission of Christ and bearing witness to him might bring upon believers the same hostility that had sent Jesus to the cross. In throwing in his lot with the church he had once persecuted, he renounced everything he had formerly prized. The purpose of this great renunciation he summed up in a few words when he stated the goal of his life in Christ:

> That I may know him and the power of his resurrection, and may share his sufferings, becoming like him in his death, that if possible I may attain to the resurrection of the dead. (Philippians 3:10-11)

Here again he used the Greek term which earlier English versions translated as "the fellowship of his sufferings," that is, literally participating in such sufferings as Christ himself had been willing to endure as he pursued to the end the goal of his saving work.

The goal on which Paul's own gaze was trained, he also held before his readers, in an earnest appeal to their "participation in the Spirit" or, in the version of 1611, "fellowship of the Spirit." Urging them to be of one mind and to practice mutual love, he went on to plead:

> Do nothing from selfishness or conceit, but in humility count others better than yourselves. Let each of you look not only to his own interests, but also to the interests of others. Have this mind among yourselves, which you have in Christ Jesus. . . . (Philippians 2:3-5)

The mind of Christ in such matters was revealed by what he did. Taking the form of a servant, he humbled himself and became obedient even to the point of dying on a cross. That was why God highly exalted him and bestowed on him the name which is above every name, so that every tongue should confess that Jesus Christ is Lord, giving glory to God the Father. Thus the roots of Christian fellowship are traced back to the death and resurrection of Jesus Christ our Lord.

The profundity and richness of this experience is indicated by this affirmation of the vocation of Christians:

> God is faithful, by whom you were called into the fellowship of his Son, Jesus Christ our Lord. (I Corinthians 1:9)

While this vocation of believers included personal fellowship with Christ himself, this was not something that could be had in isolation from others. It involved what the Latin Vulgate here called the *societas* of God's Son, the community of people of which he is Lord; the body of which he is the Head.

This sense of community is vividly expressed where the word "fellowship" is connected with the common meals shared by all members of the church as the outward sign of their unity in Christ. Thus Paul could say of the Lord's supper:

The cup of blessing which we bless, is it not a participation in the blood of Christ? The bread which we break, is it not a participation in the body of Christ? Because there is one loaf, we who are many are one body, for we all partake of the same loaf. (I Corinthians 10:16-17)

In place of the word "participation" here, earlier English versions used "communion," but it is still the same Greek term, which means "sharing" or "partnership" or "fellowship." Any idea of private communion with Christ that did not also involve real and active participation in the life and work of the Christian community was totally unthinkable in the New Testament.

One Body, Many Members

Never has Christian fellowship been pictured more graphically than when Paul wrote, ". . . we who are many are one body." It is true that Greek and Roman philosophers, before and after Paul's time, drew similar comparisons between the ideal of a well-ordered society and the cooperation that can be seen among different parts of the human body. But there is no evidence that Paul was directly influenced by any of them. They were talking about forms of society which are natural to all men everywhere: city, state, or nation. Paul was describing something so rare among men that it must be termed "supernatural," a special creation by God himself. In the world then, as now, membership in a particular race or class set a man apart from members of another race or class and often brought him into conflict with them. But the "body" of which Paul was speaking actually had as its "members" people who were drawn from many different races or classes. For it was the body of Christ, into which men were incorporated by the gift of his Spirit sent from God.

All this is implicit in that picture which Paul held up before the eyes of the Corinthian congregation in order to warn them that in God's plan there should be no schism or division in the body, and to remind them that in Christ they were all one:

For by one Spirit we were all baptized into one body—Jews or Greeks, slaves or free—and all were made to drink of one Spirit. (I Corinthians 12:13)

Outside this fellowship, fierce rivalry brought Jews and Greeks into contempt for one another. It was expressed by calling each other names: the Jew called the Greek a "Gentile" or heathen; the Greek called the Jew or any other foreigner a "barbarian." Similarly the Roman patrician looked down on the plebeian, and the empire was always troubled by the threat of revolt among the large numbers of slaves on whose labor its economy was based.

Paul's picture of the human body was a realistic one, even though he put it to symbolic use. He described a living organism with limbs and organs, each having highly specialized functions necessary to the well-being of the whole. There were the eyes, specially adapted to seeing, ears for hearing, an organ with a sense of smell. So too, hands and feet each capable of their particular work. None of these can get along without the rest, not even the head which is endowed with special abilities for direction and co-ordination. While some parts of the body seem weaker than others, they cannot be dispensed with. And those that seem unpresentable are treated with greater modesty. In fact, God has adjusted the body in such a way that if one part suffers, the whole body suffers.

With these observations Paul reached the point which he wished to drive home to the Corinthian congregation. The unity of the body of Christ is a unity in which there is rich diversity, not rigid uniformity. The community which his Spirit creates is not to be thought of as an efficient organization, like that of an army in which the highest ranking officer hands down orders to his subordinates, who in turn see that the commands are carried out with unquestioning obedience by the rank and file. Of course, its members are called into common loyalty to Christ their Lord, but it is his love that unites them in love for one another. God has "mixed together"—that is the meaning of the Greek word translated "adjusted"—this body of people with bonds of "sympathy," so that "if one member suffers, all suffer together; if one member is honored, all rejoice together."

Like the members of the human organism, the members of this Christian community are characterized more by differences than by exact likenesses. Even these differences have been given to them by God himself. In his wise and generous outpouring of the Spirit, he has endowed some with one ability, others with another, and has assigned to each his peculiar task. But his gifts are given to each man, not for his private profit, but for the common good of all. So no member can deny that he is a part of the body, nor can any single member make the presumptuous claim that his function in the body is the only all-important one. No member can say to any other member, "I don't need you!" They are all mutually interdependent. In fact, in this community a weaker or apparently less honorable member often is given special care and consideration.

All this was sharply etched by Paul in clear and bold strokes as he drew his picture of what it means to the believer to be "in Christ." Only Paul did not generalize, or leave the matter vaguely impersonal. He put it squarely on the heart of each man and woman who would hear his letter read to the congregation when next it met: "You," he said, speaking first in the plural and referring to the whole assembly, "are the body of Christ and"—then making it personal—"individually members of it." (I Corinthians 12:27) In a later letter Paul gave this thought a new and striking turn at the end:

> For as in one body we have many members, and all the members do not have the same function, so we, though many, are one body in Christ, and individually members one of another. (Romans 12:4-5)

It is a sobering and inspiring thought. Christians, as members of one great community of faith and love, belong to one another just as completely as different limbs and organs of the same body belong to one another. In a human organism, severance of a limb means a crippling of the body, but for the "member" it means death! Paul did not make this point, but a similar point was made in a later New Testament writing, in the allegory of Christ as the true vine of which his disciples are the branches. (John 15:1-11)

The Apostolic Ministry

In three books of the New Testament—Romans, First Corinthians, and Ephesians—what is said about the unity of the body is directly related to what may be called the Christian "ministry." The terms "minister" and "ministry" are used in the New Testament in the sense of "servant" and "service." This can be seen by comparing older with more recent English versions of Romans 12:7. In this sense of one who performs a service, every disciple of Christ was called to be a "minister," just as Jesus himself came not to be served, but to serve others. (Mark 10:43-45)

In the early church there were many varieties of ministry, but the ability and willingness to serve were thought of as a direct gift from God to every man and woman who had received the Spirit of his Son. So Paul wrote concerning these "spiritual gifts":

Now there are varieties of gifts, but the same Spirit; and there are varieties of service, but the same Lord; and there are varieties of working, but it is the same God who inspires them all in every one. (I Corinthians 12:4-6)

Then he went on to enumerate some of these different gifts and services and workings. There was the utterance of wisdom and of knowledge. There were gifts of healing, working of miracles, prophecy, and a peculiar type of inspiration known as "speaking with tongues," as well as the ability to interpret what was said.

The list was obviously not intended to be complete, for in other places Paul mentioned still other gifts, such as service, teaching, and exhortation. (Romans 12:6-8) All that Paul meant to point out to his readers was the fact that many different kinds of work need to be done in the church, and that some members are endowed with the ability to do one thing, some to do another. It is, as Paul said, like a body in which each limb and organ is designed to serve its own peculiar function for the good of the whole.

To the modern mind this suggests that there was a remarkably efficient "division of labor" in the early Christian community. No one seemed to expect a single "minister" to possess all the qualifications for every type of service. No individual "servant" of the congregation was called on to be preacher, teacher, pastor and administrator, all in one. On the other hand, the phrase "division of labor" is entirely inaccurate if it suggests the idea of a staff of professionally trained specialists. Least of all should it be taken to mean a well-organized system in which some one occupying an executive position at the top assigned to his various assistants their specific tasks and duties.

Careful reading of what Paul wrote about the variety of divine gifts and about their use in a Christian assembly for worship will correct such false impressions. Clearly it was God alone who, through the inspiration of the Spirit, gave to each "minister" his "orders."

God has appointed in the church first apostles, second prophets, third teachers, then workers of miracles, then healers, helpers, administrators, speakers in various kinds of tongues. Are all apostles? Are all prophets? Are all teachers? Do all work miracles? Do all possess gifts of healing? Do all speak with tongues? Do all interpret? But earnestly desire the best gifts. And I will show you a still more excellent way. (I Corinthians 12:28-31)

The best gift, the more excellent way, according to Paul, was love. Without love, speaking with tongues, prophetic powers, knowledge, and even faith itself were useless. A man might even give away everything he had and surrender his body to the awful torture of death by burning, but if such sacrifices were not prompted by genuine Christian love, nothing was gained. The characteristics of love which set it above all other gifts, according to Paul, were patience and kindness. "Love," he said, "is not jealous or boastful; it is not arrogant or rude." Nor do men moved by love insist on their own way, becoming irritable or resentful when they cannot get it. Such reminders were needed in the church at Corinth then. They are needed in every church everywhere today.

Undoubtedly, when Paul drew up such a list, he mentioned the more important services before those which were of lesser value in the life of the church. Probably the church could get along without "speaking with tongues" more readily than it could fulfill its mission to evangelize the world without the services of apostles. It could do without the working of miracles more easily than it could without teachers to nourish new converts in the faith. Paul unhesitatingly placed a far higher value on the gift of prophecy than he did on the gift of "tongues." The man who spoke in a tongue might edify himself, but he who prophesied edified the church. In that sense, he was "greater" because service to others is greatness. (I Corinthians 14:4-6)

It is hardly surprising, therefore, that in the list of gifts in Romans, Paul put prophecy at the top. What is surprising is that here he made no mention at all of the work of an apostle. (Romans 12:6-8) Attempts to explain this remarkable omission can be no more than guesses. Perhaps, at the time Paul wrote this letter to the congregation at Rome, they had never yet received the services of any apostle. But it is just as likely that none of Paul's lists was intended to be exhaustive and to cover every type of Christian ministry.

The list given in Ephesians is somewhat briefer and more precise. But although some scholars believe that this epistle was composed by someone else after Paul's time, the basic idea of the ministry was much the same. The author said that after Christ had ascended to heaven, he gave gifts to men:

> And his gifts were that some should be apostles, some prophets, some evangelists, some pastors and teachers, for the equipment of the saints, for the work of the ministry, for the building up of the body of Christ. (Ephesians 4:11-12)

Just as in Paul's first letter to Corinth, apostles and prophets head the list, while teachers are mentioned later. But before these last, two other types of ministers are added: evangelists and pastors. From the way pastors and teachers are spoken of together, it may be that the same persons performed both services.

The important point is that Christ gave to each of them different gifts, but all for the same purpose. That purpose was to equip the "saints," the people of God, for their service to him and to build them up into one body. The goal of the Christian ministry which was emphasized in the Epistle to the Ephesians was the promotion of Christian unity. This essential ministry of the church had been described by Paul in his last great appeal to the Corinthian congregation to make up the differences which had divided them into rival sects or factions. This Second Epistle to the Corinthians contained no list of separate services and functions because Paul meant to emphasize that the church's ministry is one.

Paul had affirmed that if any man is in Christ, he is a new creation. The old had passed away; the new had come:

> All this is from God, who through Christ reconciled us to himself and gave us the ministry of reconciliation; that is, God was in Christ

reconciling the world to himself, not counting their trespasses against them, and entrusting to us the message of reconciliation. So we are ambassadors for Christ, God making his appeal through us. We beseech you on behalf of Christ, be reconciled to God. (II Corinthians 5:18-20)

This, according to Paul, was the "apostolic" ministry to which God had called him. But not him alone. Paul did not say "me," he said "us." This would include, of course, Timothy, whose name was associated with Paul's at the beginning of the letter. But it would include his readers at Corinth, too. As Christians they were people whom God had reconciled to himself by the forgiveness of their sins through Christ. Having granted them his peace, he had given them a service to perform. They were to carry his "message of reconciliation" to the world. As Christ's ambassadors they were to appeal to men to accept peace from God.

When men are reconciled to God they can have peace with one another and enter into the unity of the body of Christ. That is the message of the Epistle to the Ephesians. The author reminded his readers that at one time, when they were Gentiles, they had been separated from Christ, alienated from the commonwealth of Israel, having no hope and without God in the world. But Christ came and proclaimed God's peace to Jew and Gentile alike. He united believers from both groups after breaking down the wall of hostility between them and abolishing the old requirements of the law. So he had made peace, reconciling both Jewish and Gentile believers to God in one body, through his death on the cross. Together, those once divided in the world could at last approach their Father with confidence, in the unity of the Spirit. (Ephesians 2:11-18)

In a world torn apart by jealousy and suspicion, fear and hate, Paul recognized the "ministry of reconciliation" as the essential ministry of the church. The Christians of his day were imperfect Christians, and their very human faults and failings threatened to rend the unity of the body. It is not difficult to imagine with what mingled shock and sadness he wrote to the congregation at Corinth, "When you assemble as a church, I hear that there are divisions among you." (I Corinthians 11:18) If that were the case, he had to tell them that when they came together, it was not for the better but for the worse. For the purpose for which they were called to assemble was to worship God in one Spirit, by which they had all been baptized into one body, and to break together the one loaf of the Lord's supper. These were the signs of their oneness in Christ, and the means of deepening and strengthening their sense of brotherhood under God.

Worship in the Spirit

Instructions for the proper conduct of meetings for worship are much more scanty in the New Testament than in the Christian literature of later centuries. One reason for this lack of detailed instruction was the freedom and spontaneity with which the earliest believers offered their praise to God as they were inspired by the Holy Spirit. The services in those first "house-churches" presented a striking contrast to the fixed forms and ceremonies which were a marked feature in the temple worship of Judaism, as well as of other ancient religions.

A story in the fourth gospel suggests a similar contrast. Jesus met a woman of Samaria who tried to engage him in a long-standing controversy between her people and the Jews: where was the right place to worship God? Centuries earlier the Samaritans had built their own temple on Mount Gerizim, only to have it destroyed by invading Jewish armies in the second century before Christ. For the Jews interpreted the law as limiting sacrificial worship to the sanctuary at Jerusalem. In answer to the woman's question, Jesus replied that the time would come when people would no longer worship God on that mountain in Samaria, nor in Jerusalem. (By the time the fourth gospel was written the temple there too had been destroyed.) Then he added:

> The hour is coming, and now is, when the true worshippers will worship the Father in spirit and truth, for such the Father seeks to worship him. God is spirit, and those who worship him must worship in spirit and truth. (John 4:23-24)

The true spirit of worship cannot be limited to any single locality or day, but God's children should give thanks to him at all times and in all places. God is spirit, everywhere present and near to his people wherever they may be. All that matters to him is that their devotion should be offered with sincerity and in reality. It is such worshippers that the Father seeks.

Paul firmly believed that the initiative in Christian worship always came from God, rather than from men. It was God who sent the Spirit of his Son into the hearts of believers, enabling them to call him by the very name which Jesus had used in prayer. That name was "Abba," the Aramaic word for Father. (Mark 14:36; Romans 8:15; Galatians 4:6) Since men do not know how to pray as they ought, the Spirit helps them in their weakness with intercessions that cannot be expressed in words. (Romans 8:26-27) Paul went so far as to say that no one can confess Jesus as Lord except by the Holy Spirit, and included faith among the gifts of God. (I Corinthians 12:3, 9)

It was this kind of Spirit-inspired worship that Paul described in the long chapter on prophecy and "speaking with tongues," in which he wrote:

> When you come together, each one has a hymn, a lesson, a revelation, a tongue, or an interpretation. Let all things be done for edification. If any speak in a tongue, let there be only two or at most three, and each in turn; and let one interpret. . . . (I Corinthians 14:26-27)

This was a warning that no gift nor the liberty of using it should be abused. If every member of the congregation in a sudden burst of inspiration were to speak at once, an unbeliever hearing them would suppose they were madmen. So each member must exercise self-control. For God is not a God of confusion but of peace. Yet Paul would not have any one in the congregation forbid others to speak in tongues. Christian discipline should be self-discipline. Only he concluded, "All things should be done decently and in order." (I Corinthians 14:40)

Paul's advice in this regard indicates that he wished the meetings of the congregation to continue, as before, in unpremeditated responsiveness to the leading of the Holy Spirit. Had he considered it wise or necessary to repress all such spontaneous enthusiasm, he could easily have instructed the Corinthians to organize their assembly after the familiar pattern of the Jewish synagogues. This might have included the election or appointment of a chairman to keep order. To him would have been entrusted the assignment of prayers and other parts of the service to the various members of the church who were to participate on any given day. Paul's direct appeal to all members of the congregation to observe suitable order and decorum makes it clear that there was as yet no such presiding officer at gatherings of the church in Corinth, although the time was coming when this would be the case. Whatever the gifts of the "administrators" of whom Paul speaks in this letter, their function was evidently not the same as that of the Jewish "rulers of the synagogue." Probably they were entrusted with the management of the charitable funds and services of the community.

Yet the Christian church does appear to have inherited from earliest times two practices of the Jewish assemblies. First, members of the congregation were expected to participate in the acts of worship. This raises the question whether the limitation of "membership" to adult males, which was the rule in Judaism, likewise prevailed in early Christianity. Paul's statement, "the women should keep silence in the churches," has been understood in this way. (I Corinthians 14:34) But this cannot possibly have meant that the inspiration of the Spirit was denied them, or that they were forbidden to speak when inspired to do so. For before giving his instructions about the Lord's supper, Paul offered some advice about "any woman who prays or prophesies with her head unveiled." (I Corinthians 11:5) This certainly implied that a woman suitably attired might take active part in the church's worship.

Second, there was recognition that a primary place in worship must be given to the word of God. The apostles, prophets, teachers, and evangelists all exercised "the ministry of the word." Through this ministry the church continued to live and grow, because "faith comes by what is heard, and what is heard comes by the preaching of Christ." (Romans 10:17) Paul emphasized this ministry in describing his own commission as an apostle, by saying: "Christ did not send me to baptize but to preach the gospel." (I Corinthians 1:17) Of course, this did not mean that Paul placed a low value on baptism, but simply that he knew that without evangelism, without the preaching of the saving gospel, there would have been no believers to receive baptism.

Baptism and the Lord's Supper

In Paul's letters, baptism and the Lord's supper were closely related to the doctrine that believers are members of the body of Christ. It was by the one Spirit that they were all baptized into that one body. (I Corinthians 12:13) Although repentance is not specifically mentioned by Paul in this connection, other evidence indicates that from earliest times such a turning away from sin was always required of converts, who were then baptized "in the name of Jesus Christ." (Acts 2:38) Paul said simply that they were baptized "into Christ." (Romans 6:3; Galatians 3:27) This meant not only that they acknowledged him as their Lord, but that they were so intimately joined to him that they were said to have "put on Christ." Thus they were incorporated into his living body, the whole company of faithful people. Later, as the theology of the church developed, baptism came to be administered "in the name of the Father and of the Son and of the Holy Spirit."

Baptism with the Holy Spirit was often contrasted with the earlier practice of John the Baptist, who baptized with water only. (Mark 1:8; Acts 1:5) When Paul came to Ephesus, he found there a group of twelve disciples who had never even heard of the Holy Spirit, having received John's baptism. After further instruction, they were baptized in the name of the Lord Jesus, and after Paul laid his hands on them the Holy Spirit came on them, inspiring them to speak with tongues and prophesy. (Acts 19:1-7) Curiously enough, there was an instance in which even people who were baptized in the name of the Lord Jesus failed to receive the Holy Spirit, which was later given them through the laying on of hands by the apostles Peter and John. (Acts 8:14-17) But there was no invariable norm. Sometimes the gift of the Spirit was reported to have followed immediately after baptism; in other cases, the Spirit was given first, with baptism administered afterward. (Acts 2:38; 10:44-47) What mattered in any case was that believers should be filled with the Holy Spirit, for "any one who does not have the Spirit of Christ does not belong to him." (Romans 8:9)

Since the Greek verb which has given us our word "baptize" means "to dip" or "to immerse" oneself in water, its earliest associations were with the need for cleansing, often in a physical sense. The Septuagint used this verb in the story which told how Naaman the Syrian was cleansed of his leprosy by dipping himself seven times in the river Jordan. (II Kings 5:9-14) Paul described believers as having been "washed," as well as consecrated, in the name of Jesus Christ and in the Spirit of God. (I Corinthians 6:11) Here he referred specifically to a cleansing from former heathen vices. In another letter Paul's description of the radical break with the old life of sin, symbolized in baptism, is even more graphic. As the new convert to Christ descended below the water, he was vividly reminded of the death and burial of Christ himself. Then as he was raised from the water, his re-emergence became the sign of resurrection to new life with God. Thus to be baptized means to be "dead to sin and alive to God in Christ Jesus." (Romans 6:3-11)

The Lord's supper likewise was closely connected with Paul's doctrine that believers are to share in Christ's death. The phrase "fellowship of his sufferings" is a more general expression, while "participation in the blood of Christ" is a more specific statement of the same truth. (Philippians 3:10; I Corinthians 10:16) Yet when Paul goes on to speak of "participation in the body of Christ," it is clear that he has in mind their unity as members of a living organism. (I Corinthians 10:17)

The nature of the common meal regularly shared by the members of the Christian community shines through the words which Paul had to write to the Corinthians to correct their misuse of it. What should have taken place is clear enough. The congregation assembled in the home of one of its members, waiting until all had gathered. Probably each contributed such food as he could, but all shared alike. Before they partook of the cup, a blessing was addressed to God. A similar offering of thanks accompanied the breaking of the loaf of bread. As they shared these simple elements of food, their minds were carried back to the last meal which Jesus had eaten with his disciples, and the solemn words he had then spoken were perhaps repeated. As often as they ate this bread and drank of the cup, they proclaimed the Lord's death for them, and would continue to do so until the day when he would come again. Yet even at that moment they knew that he was with them, for his Spirit breathed through each of them, inspiring every word and action in their worship. By the unity of the Spirit, they were one body, Christ's body.

What had actually happened at Corinth to call forth Paul's

rebuke was something very different from this. In the first place, reports had reached him that there were divisions in the congregation. If this were so, as he had reason to believe, their coming together was not for the better, but for the worse. So, he continued, it was not really the Lord's supper that they ate, because each individual went ahead with his own meal, without waiting for others. The result was that some of those who arrived later went away hungry, while others became drunken. Paul could only conclude that such people had no respect for the congregation of God, since they humiliated their poorer brothers who had nothing.

It was at this point that Paul reminded them of the tradition which he had delivered to them during his stay in Corinth, a tradition which they had evidently forgotten or failed to understand:

> For I received from the Lord what I also delivered to you, that the Lord Jesus on the night when he was betrayed took bread, and when he had given thanks, he broke it, and said, 'This is my body which is for you. Do this in remembrance of me.' In the same way also the cup, after supper, saying, 'This cup is the new covenant in my blood. Do this, as often as you drink it, in remembrance of me.' (I Corinthians 11:23-25)

This is the earliest written account of the last supper that has come down to us, and while the first three gospel records differ in some of the details, the main points are the same. Especially to be noted is the reference to the covenant which has been sealed by the shedding of Christ's blood.

Among the evangelists, Luke alone shared with Paul the tradition that Jesus had instructed the disciples, "Do this in remembrance of me," thereby insuring the continued observance of the supper. However, some ancient texts of our third gospel omitted this part of the narrative, as can be seen from the latest revision of the English version. (Luke 22:19-20) Mark reported that Jesus had spoken of his blood as "poured out for many," to which

Matthew added that this was done "for the forgiveness of sins." Otherwise there was substantial agreement in the four accounts which are contained in the New Testament.

Other Variations in the Traditions

The fourth evangelist reflects a different line of tradition regarding both baptism and the last supper. His is the only gospel to report that baptism was already practiced among the disciples of Jesus during his earthly ministry. It is not clear whether he actually intended to state that Jesus himself ever baptized anyone. Possibly the parenthesis which corrects such an impression was added by a later editor. (John 3:22; 4:1-3) It is in this gospel, too, that Jesus is reported to have said to Nicodemus, "Unless one is born of water and the Spirit, he cannot enter the kingdom of God." (John 3:5) These words are generally understood to refer to Christian baptism, to distinguish it from the baptism with water only, as practiced by John the Baptist. (John 1:31) Later, baptism came to be called "the washing of regeneration and renewal in the Holy Spirit." (Titus 3:5)

In the Gospel according to John, it is the meal which Jesus shared with the multitude in the wilderness, rather than the final supper in the upper room, which introduces the teaching that Christ himself is "the bread of life." The following day, at Capernaum, some of those who had eaten of the broken bread reminded Jesus of the manna in the wilderness, calling it by a scriptural phrase, "bread from heaven." (John 6:31; Psalm 105:40) But when Jesus identified himself as the bread which came down from heaven, some of the more literal-minded Jews objected, "How can this man give us his flesh to eat?" To such people the mystery of Christ's true origin could not be revealed, though it was reiterated that only by feeding on Christ can men have eternal life. Afterward, Jesus is reported to have said to his disciples, "It is the spirit that gives life, the flesh is of no

avail. The words that I have spoken to you are spirit and life."
(John 6:63) The evangelist leaves every reader to ponder over
the significance of this revelation of the mind of Christ.

The narrative of the last supper, on the night before the crucifixion, contains a profoundly significant lesson in the record of
this evangelist. Luke had recorded that while Jesus sat at the
table with his disciples, a dispute had arisen among them about
which one was to be regarded as the greatest. Then Jesus had
said to them:

> For which is the greater, one who sits at table, or one who serves?
> Is not the one who sits at table? But I am among you as one who
> serves. (Luke 22:27)

As if to supplement this saying, the fourth evangelist related how
Jesus had put its intention into action. Laying aside his outer
garments, and girding himself with a towel, Jesus had gone from
one disciple to the next, doing the lowly task of a household
slave, as he washed the disciples' feet. Here, too, a symbolic reference to baptism as an act of cleansing has been suggested by
some interpreters of the gospel. Yet the lesson to be drawn
from this act of Jesus is contained in these words:

> You call me Teacher and Lord; and you are right, for so I am. If
> I then, your Lord and Teacher, have washed your feet, you also
> ought to wash one another's feet. For I have given you an example,
> that you should do as I have done to you. Truly, truly, I say to you,
> a servant is not greater than his master, nor is he who is sent greater
> than he who sent him. If you know these things, happy are you if
> you do them. (John 13:13-17)

Moreover, the example to which the gospel points is the whole
life of Christ among men, which culminated in his great act of
love in laying down his life for them. To such sacrificial love
every disciple is called:

> A new commandment I give to you, that you love one another;
> even as I have loved you, that you also love one another. By this

all men will know that you are my disciples, if you have love for one another. (John 13:34-35)

Through the succeeding centuries the church was to develop further its distinctive doctrines and institutions, its ministry and sacraments, its discipline and worship, together with varying tests of membership. But it would never advance beyond this "new commandment." Disciples of Christ are to be recognized by deeds of love like his.

CHAPTER FOUR

THE CHURCH AND THE WORLD

THROUGH the labors of wise master builders like Paul, as well as of many fellow workers not even named in the records, the new temple continued to rise—not a structure of bricks and mortar —rather "a spiritual house" composed of "living stones," the lives of people joined together in unity of faith and purpose. The "cornerstone" of their fellowship was Christ himself. Against a house so built, neither the storms of life nor the power of death could prevail.

Yet faith in Christ crucified did not permit such people to seek their own safety in sanctuary while others were perishing. Jesus had warned that discipleship meant discipline, rather than easy escape from the risks of living: "Whoever would save his life will lose it; and whoever loses his life for my sake and the gospel's will save it." (Mark 8:35)

The church was not called by God to become an end in itself, but the means of bearing the good news of his reconciling love to the world. Its members were not allowed to sit "at ease in Zion," enjoying the peace of God in selfish isolation from the rest of humanity. As Christ's ambassadors, they were to make known to all men everywhere that he is Lord of life. He had sent them, by the authority given him by the Father, to make disciples of all nations. They were to go out as his witnesses, to build God's temple—not only in Jerusalem or Samaria, but also at Antioch and Ephesus, in Corinth and far distant Rome. Every city was to be made a "holy city" because it was inhabited by the "saints," the people of God!

Since this was the church's mission to the world, Paul's metaphor of the "building" was less appropriate than his other word picture of "the body." A building suggests something fixed and static. A body is an organism that lives and grows. The church could be called the body of Christ, only if it was filled with his Spirit, without which it would cease to live. Led by the Holy Spirit, who is called the Spirit of truth, the apostolic church became what it was intended to be, Christ's witness to the world. (Mark 13:9-11; John 15:26-27; Acts 1:8)

Witnesses to the People

Few words describe the mission of the first disciples more clearly than the words "witness," "testimony," and "testify," which Luke used in recording one event after another in the Acts of the Apostles. A witness is a person who can give reliable evidence of a fact of which he has personal knowledge. His testimony to the truth is something he ought not hold back. To keep silence would be no better than to bear false witness. As Peter and John said to the high priest and council: "We cannot but speak of what we have seen and heard." (Acts 4:20) Those earliest Christians did not think this obligation was limited to testifying in court. They were to be Christ's witnesses to the people, testifying to all men, both great and small, Gentiles as well as Jews. (Acts 13:31; 20:21; 22:15; 23:11; 26:22)

The disciples of Jesus had learned how to bear witness by deeds as well as words, and to seize every opportunity to make known the healing power of their Master. What are called "medical missions" were not a recent invention, even though modern methods differ from those of ancient times. Luke recorded how often the apostolic missionaries first showed concern for people's physical disabilities and diseases, before attempting to do the work of evangelists. A lame man begging for alms was given something better. In the name of Jesus Christ he was given power to walk. (Acts 3:6)

Missionary opportunities were discovered even in adverse circumstances. The scattering of the disciples from Jerusalem through persecution was recognized as a call from God to proclaim Christ in other places, among the Samaritans, or to a chance traveler on a desert road to Gaza. Stephen, the first Christian martyr, bore witness even while he was dying. In fact, the word *martyr* is simply the Greek term meaning "a witness." Among the Jews who consented to the stoning of Stephen was Saul of Tarsus. What he saw that day must have left an unforgettable impression: this disciple of Jesus, Stephen, facing death not only with faith and courage, but with a prayer of forgiveness for his persecutors. Such an experience may well have prepared the way for the conversion of Saul the church's persecutor, to Paul the apostle of Christ.

The witnesses found themselves going to strange places to tell the story of Jesus to people they would normally have avoided. A Jew like Peter had to overcome long ingrained religious scruples before he was willing to venture into the house of a Roman centurion at Caesarea. But having taken the step, Peter had to see it through, speaking with such fervor that his Gentile hearers caught the Spirit. Later, when called upon to defend his action, Peter was able to persuade the rest of the apostles and brethren at Jerusalem that God had granted the Gentiles the opportunity for repentance and the gift of new life in Christ.

In his missionary journeys to the great centers of the Hellenistic world, Paul made a regular practice of visiting the Jewish synagogues where he would be permitted to address the congregation. Often this gave him an opportunity to testify not only to Jews, but also to Gentile "God fearers" who attended the meetings on the sabbath. When opposition arose in the synagogue at Ephesus, Paul is reported to have secured the use of "the school of Tyrannus" in which he continued to teach for a period of two years. This "school" was probably a philosophical lecture hall which the owners were willing to rent to Paul at times when it was not needed for their own use. Similarly, at Athens Paul is said to have spoken to a crowd of people which gathered at the Areopagus, a kind of public forum.

Such meetings must have been very informal, and the apostolic preaching was often punctuated with interruptions. Few persons in the audience would hesitate about shouting questions or objections, just as they were accustomed to do with the street-corner preachers of the Stoic and Cynic moralities. Sometimes the crowd might simply drift away in disinterest. At other times the meeting would break up with loud arguments, and even with violence. Then the preachers might be dragged before the local magistrates, charged with disturbing the peace. After a severe beating they would be thrown into jail for the night.

The more zealous Christian witnesses were not to be silenced by trial or imprisonment. Given an opportunity to testify in court, they preached the gospel to their judges. In prison they prayed and sang hymns, and soon had the other prisoners listening to their message. They might even convert the jailor, as Paul and Silas are reported to have done at Philippi.

Both the book of Acts and the collection of Paul's letters have tended to create the impression that he was the chief, if not quite the only, pioneer in the evangelization of the Roman world. Yet there is mute evidence to show that the growth of the church depended on the unsung labors of many others whose names were soon forgotten. The New Testament failed to record the actual founding of several of the most influential churches located in principal cities of the empire, such as Alexandria and Rome. Luke knew that when Apollos, a Jew born in Alexandria, came to Ephesus, he was already accurately informed about Jesus. If

Apollos had obtained this information in his native city, there may have been a Christian congregation there as early as A.D. 50. It was not until the fourth century that a legend was recorded claiming Mark, the author of the gospel, as the founder of the Alexandrian church.

The origins of the church at Rome are equally obscure. When Paul came to Corinth in A.D. 50, he met there a fellow Jew, Aquila of Pontus, who with his wife Priscilla had recently left Italy because the emperor Claudius had ordered all Jews out of Rome. The biographer Suetonius, in his life of Claudius, stated that the Emperor expelled the Jews because of riots connected with the name of "Chrestus." Since this name was sometimes confused with "Christus," it might be that the tumults were caused by some argument about the Messiah. However, the name of Jesus was apparently unknown to Suetonius. Aquila and Priscilla soon became Paul's associates in the work of evangelism, which suggests that they were already Christians, perhaps before leaving Rome. At any rate, there was a Christian congregation in that city a few years later when Paul wrote his letter to the Romans, about A.D. 56. It is impossible to believe that Paul, who knew Peter intimately, would have failed to mention his name in this letter if he had been in Rome by that time. A popular opinion that Peter and Paul were together in Rome "preaching the gospel and founding the church" was first mentioned by Irenaeus, bishop of Lyons, about A.D. 180, and has very little to support it.

In spite of the uncertainty of the record, and in spite of oppositions from Jews and pagans, the gospel made its progress from city to city across the empire to its capital. As the church sought to invade the world with the spirit of Christ, the spirit of the world often managed to invade the church, reasserting the old divisions and rivalries between Jew and Greek, slave and freeman. Moreover, the world struck back in violent attack, in a vain effort to end forever the fellowship of the Spirit, just as its rulers had tried to put an end to the mission of Jesus by nailing him to a cross. In the midst of the dangers which beset the Christian community as it strove to stand before the world as a faithful witness to Christ, its leaders had to grapple with a number of perplexing problems which arose to disturb its members, even to the point of straining their fellowship. A problem of immediate consideration for all Jewish Christians, as well as for many Gentile converts who recognized in the Hebrew scriptures a revelation from God, was how far believers in the gospel were obligated to obey the laws attributed to Moses.

The Law and the Gospel

Jesus was believed to have come to fulfill the law and the prophets. Yet the law and its faithful fulfillment among pious Jews had always included more than the observance of the religious and moral duties laid down in the ten commandments. The same scriptures which forbade adultery, murder, stealing, and bearing false witness, contained lists of "unclean animals" not to be eaten as food, ritual for the "purifying" of a woman after childbirth and for the circumcision of a male child on the eighth day. (Leviticus 11:1-12:8) A good Jew believed that neglect of any of these rules was a sin against God's will. Although Jesus had eaten with publicans and sinners, and his disciples were criticized for neglecting the Pharisean tradition about washing their hands before meals, long afterward Peter could still protest against visiting a Gentile household: "I have never eaten anything that is common or unclean." (Acts 10:14)

Since Gentiles could become proselytes to Judaism, the possibility of their conversion to Christianity must have been admitted from the beginning. The chief problem would have been on what terms they might be admitted to fellowship with Jewish believers. From Paul's letters we have firsthand evidence concerning the questions which arose. In a letter to the churches of Galatia, in Asia Minor, he had occasion to review the history of his own relations with the leaders of the church at Jerusalem, especially with regard to his mission to the Gentiles.

Many years after his call to be an apostle, he had gone to Jerusalem with Barnabas, taking along a Greek Christian named Titus. Although he was a Gentile, this disciple was not compelled to be circumcised, in spite of some men whom Paul described as "false brethren" who slipped into the meeting with that intention. When he wrote, ". . . to them we did not yield submission," Paul obviously included Barnabas with himself. But since he reported that James, Cephas, and John—reputed "pillars" of the church at Jerusalem—gave him and Barnabas "the right hand of fellowship," it is probable that they too resisted any demand for the circumcision of Gentile Christians. At least there was common agreement that Paul and Barnabas should continue their work among the Gentiles, while the apostles at Jerusalem devoted themselves to the evangelization of their fellow Jews. (Galatians 2:1-10)

Unfortunately this accord failed to settle the matter. Paul recalled with mingled disappointment and disapproval the wavering conduct of Cephas, the Aramaic name by which he usually spoke of Peter. At first, when Cephas came to Antioch, he had eaten with the Gentiles. But when certain men came from James, he drew back and separated himself from such fellowship, through fear of the circumcision party. This led other Jewish Christians at Antioch, including even Barnabas, to refuse to share a meal with Gentile Christians. Although Paul did not specifically say so, this probably meant that there had to be separate celebrations of the Lord's supper and the unity of the body was broken. (Galatians 2:11-13)

For such behavior, Paul said he opposed Cephas to his face because he stood condemned. What troubled Paul was that these Jewish Christians apparently wished to compel Gentile Christians to live like Jews. Against this Paul affirmed the conviction that "a man is not justified by works of the law but through faith in Jesus

Christ." If it were otherwise, then Christ had died in vain. The issue, as Paul saw it, was clear. Either a man had to try to earn God's favor by keeping the law in its smallest details—a way Paul had tried without success as a Pharisee; or he could accept God's love and merciful forgiveness as a gift freely given in Christ. This gift, which is what Paul meant by "grace," he had experienced since his conversion to faith in Jesus. He had died to the law, in order that he might live to God. From that time on he was a new and different man, living by faith in the Son of God, who had given himself for him in an act of pure love. This gift, humbly accepted in gratitude to the Giver, had provided Paul with a new source of spiritual and moral power. The same gift was freely offered to every believer. (Galatians 2:15-20)

At the time that Paul reviewed these events, he had been surprised and angered by the report that someone was preaching "a different gospel"—which was not a true gospel at all—in the churches of Galatia. Gentile converts there were being told that they must accept circumcision, a rite which obligated them to keep the whole law. Paul's protest against this perversion of the Christian message was vigorous and blunt: "For freedom Christ has set us free; stand fast therefore and do not submit again to a yoke of slavery." He denied that either circumcision or the lack of it counted for anything. All that really mattered was that a man should become a "new creation" in Christ. (Galatians 5:1-6; 6:11-15)

Yet Paul was careful to point out to his Gentile readers that genuine Christian liberty must not be mistaken for moral license, a life without restraint. The believer should be guided in all that he did by the Spirit of Christ, rather than by his natural desires and appetites. The "fruit" which the Spirit produced in the life of the Christian would be love, joy, peace, patience, kindness, self-control, and other kindred virtues. Against such dispositions and habits as these, there could be no law. (Galatians 5:16-23)

Paul's successful struggle against the Judaizers offered the first

assurance that the Christian church would become truly "catholic" in the original sense of that term, "universal." If his opponents could have had their way, Christians would have remained
a small exclusive Jewish sect, in which few if any Greeks or
Romans would have found admission. Like the Pharisean "separatists," they might have tried to maintain a false conception of
"holiness" in a purely ritual sense, and interpreted their "election"
from God as a private privilege, rather than a responsibility for
bringing his light to all the world.

Yet the church's rapid growth among the Gentiles was accompanied by other serious threats to its true character, and once
again Paul was quick to sense the danger and to sound the alarm.
His first letter to the Corinthians is a record of the peril that the
spirit of worldliness and paganism might engulf the church if its
members remained only half converted to the genuine Spirit of
Christ.

The famous seaport and commercial center of Corinth was
known proverbially, even among pagans, as a place where immorality flourished. Yet Paul was shocked to learn that some of
his converts there were living lives which he believed no decent
pagan would condone. Had Paul believed that the Old Testament
legal codes were binding on Christians, he could have quoted
their prohibitions, "a man shall not take his father's wife." (Deuteronomy 22:30) But Paul was no legalist. Still his judgment and
the punishment he advised was severe, for the offender must be
dismissed from the fellowship, although Paul held out the hope
that his spirit might ultimately be saved. (I Corinthians 5:1-5)

In this case Paul's rebuke fell heavily on the whole congregation since they showed no evidence of corporate penitence for the
evil in their midst, but had grown arrogant. He would have them
realize that just as a little leaven ferments the whole lump of
dough, so the wrongdoing of a few members could destroy the effectiveness of the church's witness to the world. Paul was realistic
enough to know that Christians cannot withdraw from the

world, nor did he feel called to judge the behavior of outsiders. They could be left to God. The church must clean its own house. (I Corinthians 5:6-13) In this respect each individual member had a responsibility to live an exemplary life. "Do you not know," asked Paul, "that your body is a temple of the Holy Spirit within you, which you have from God? You are not your own; you were bought with a price. So glorify God in your body." (I Corinthians 6:19)

Further evidence that worldliness had invaded the church at Corinth was seen in disputes between its members. Instead of settling their grievances out of court, one brother hailed another before pagan judges. If there was no one in the congregation wise enough to decide such cases, Paul said it would be better for a man to endure the wrong than to run the risk of inflicting a wrong on his brother. (I Corinthians 6:1-8) The man who gave that advice had learned the essential difference between the law and the gospel in the school of Jesus. (Matthew 5:38-42)

Another difficult problem for Christians living in any pagan city was what to do about food offered to idols. With the vast number of daily sacrifices in the various pagan temples, such "dedicated" food was offered for sale in any meat market, except those specially set up by Jews for their own use. If a Christian accepted an invitation to a meal with a pagan neighbor, the food was almost certain to be of this kind. So the Corinthian congregation had written Paul, asking his advice and suggesting a solution of their own. They asserted, "All things are lawful." Paul replied this might be so, but not all things are helpful. They had boasted, "All of us possess knowledge," adding "an idol has no real existence" and "there is no God but one." Of course, Paul agreed. Yet, he pointed out, there was something more important than knowledge. That was love. Knowledge could inflate a man's ego. Only love could build up the brotherhood.

A Christian, according to Paul must not think only about himself. He must show concern for the welfare of his brothers. In this case, there might be some new convert, until recently accustomed to the worship of idols, who would eat the dedicated food as a real offering to a pagan deity, causing harm to his conscience. So a believer must take care lest by asserting his liberty from the law he should put a stumbling-block in the way of such a brother. "Therefore," Paul concluded, "if food is a cause of my brother's falling, I will never eat meat, lest I cause my brother to fall." (I Corinthians 8:13) Yet Paul regarded all food as a gift from God, to be partaken with thankfulness to him. "So, whether you eat or drink . . . do all to the glory of God. Give no offense to Jews or to Greeks or to the church of God . . ." (I Corinthians 10:31-32) The problem of eating food offered to idols, though a serious one in the early church, eventually disappeared from most of the Western world, but the spirit in which Paul met the problem has been permanently fruitful wherever followed by Christians.

The Form of This World Is Passing

Paul was a man of the first century, and the problems he had to deal with were those of his own age. Some were purely local problems which affected only a single congregation. To meet such problems Paul wrote letters, not law books. Like most letter writers, he probably expected that when his message to a particular church had served its purpose it would be destroyed. This evidently happened to an early letter which Paul mentioned having written to the congregation at Corinth. (I Corinthians 5:9) Certainly Paul had no intention that these very frank and intimate fragments of his correspondence with people he knew so well should be bound together in a permanent collection for constant reference and quotation by Christians of later ages.

The fact is that Paul, like other early disciples, firmly believed and earnestly hoped that the Lord would soon descend from heaven to gather together his people, both the living and the

dead. Paul confidently expected that he and many of his con-
temporaries would live to see that great day. (I Thessalonians
4:16-17; I Corinthians 15:51-52) As for this world, its form was
already passing away, and the appointed time had grown very
short. (I Corinthians 7:29-31) The idea that the world was des-
tined to continue through repeated historical crises for nineteen
centuries never seems to have crossed the mind of Paul or any
other Christian of his day. This is most natural when we realize
how difficult it is to imagine life on this planet even a century beyond our own time. The historical horizon of all men is severely
limited by the uncertainty of the future.

Such limitation in historical perspective inevitably affects
men's judgment with regard to the best way of ordering the com-
plex relations of human life, social, political, or economic. Looking backward, men learn that the conditions of life in the past
have changed from generation to generation. Often past changes
appear as signs of "progress." Yet men do not readily welcome
the suggestion that there must be further radical changes in their
way of life, and the conservative desire to keep things as they are
is common.

The first Christians had inherited from Judaism the unshakable
belief that God was leading his people toward a glorious future
in the life of the age to come. So Paul believed on the testimony
of scripture: "No eye has seen, nor ear heard, nor the heart of man
conceived, what God has prepared for those who love him." (I
Corinthians 2:9) However, it was a common expectation among
Jews and Christians that conditions of life in this age would grow
steadily worse before the long-awaited day of the Lord arrived.
The saints must be prepared for trial and persecution, for the evil
powers of the world would try to destroy their faith by violence.
So believers were advised not to become involved in worldly
affairs, in order to give their undivided devotion to the Lord.

This limited historical outlook lay directly behind much of the
advice which Paul gave concerning marriage to his converts at

Corinth, as well as that concerning the status of Jew and Gentile, slave and freeman. "I think," he wrote (as a matter of personal opinion, not as a command of the Lord), "that in view of the impending distress it is well for a person to remain as he is." (I Corinthians 7:26) A married man should not seek to become free from the obligations of marriage, as apparently some of the Corinthians proposed to do. On the other hand, it would be wiser for the unmarried to continue single, although Paul carefully pointed out that this did not mean marriage and the relationship between husband and wife was wrong. He merely wanted to spare converts additional anxieties.

It is obvious that advice such as this was suitable only if, as Paul believed, the appointed time until the end of the world was very short. If, on the contrary, God's purpose for this world could not be tied to the artificial timetable of certain Jewish messianic hopes, a different course would have to be followed by his people. As human history continued through succeeding centuries, the Christian community would have gone down in suicide had its members obeyed Paul's advice to the unmarried to remain so. Without marriage, and the family there could be no future for any human society, including the church itself. But Paul had never intended to lay down a law for the church, and the failure of his eschatological expectations to materialize soon rendered his advice obsolete.

In much the same way, Paul's advice as applied to other social and economic institutions of his day was very far from presenting a defense of the *status quo*. Rather it meant that within the Christian fellowship the barriers which the world had erected to separate the circumcised from the uncircumcised, the slave from the freeman, were being transcended in a higher unity. "For he who was called in the Lord as a slave is a freedman of the Lord. Likewise he who was free when called is a slave of Christ. You were bought with a price; do not become slaves of men." (I Corinthians 7:22-23) If the church in the first century failed to launch a direct attack on the institution of slavery which was so solidly intrenched in the ancient world, this did not mean that Christians took a complacent attitude toward existing social evils. Only they had no confidence in the power of violence to overthrow an evil system, knowing that bad ideas and habits can only be displaced by good ones.

Besides, the early church drew larger numbers of its members from the depressed classes of Roman society than from the aristocratic and well-to-do. As Paul reminded the Corinthians, not many of them were wise according to worldly standards, not many were powerful, not many were of noble birth. To have preached social and economic reforms to the poor, weak, and despised people who frequented the Christian assemblies would only have confirmed the suspicions of many pagans highly paced in government and business that the new movement was a threat to the order and well-being of the empire. That would have been an unwise invitation to persecution which came soon enough anyway. Yet the alternative course to which the gospel of Jesus led his followers was clearly not the way of prudent caution. It was a daring overthrow of the world's cherished standards of value.

Jesus had voiced the confident assurance that God cares for the humblest of all his creatures. Not even a sparrow falls to the ground without his knowledge; yet his human children are of more value than many sparrows. In the final judgment, the nations would be tested by their concern for the hungry, the homeless, the sick, and those in prison, for as they did to one of the least of his brethren, they did to Christ himself. (Matthew 10:29-31; 25:31-46) Within the company of his disciples there were to be no distinctions marked by titles and positions of authority on which the world set such store; among them true greatness would be found in humble service. (Matthew 20:20-27; 23:1-12) "You have one teacher, and you are all brethren."

Within the church of Paul's day this was a key that opened

many doors. The shortest, and one of the most appealing, of all his letters was written by the great apostle to the Gentiles to win a charitable welcome for a runaway slave, named Onesimus, whom Paul had converted during an imprisonment. The owner of Onesimus was likewise a Christian well-known to Paul. In his brief note to Philemon, Paul wrote that the runaway was coming home, and asked that he be received "no longer as a slave but more than a slave, as a beloved brother." (Philemon 16) When one realizes how severely any disobedient or escaped slave could be punished in the Roman world, it becomes clear how revolutionary such a request must have seemed. A Stoic moralist might suggest, as Paul did, that masters should treat their slaves justly and fairly. (Colossians 4:1) But only a Christian could remind both owners and slaves of a Master in heaven who had redeemed them from bondage at the price of his own life, a Master whose love made them sons of God and brethren.

The faith of those earliest Christians, that above the disorder and division of this world stands the eternal order of God's reign, was never by intention an obstacle of man's moral efforts to effect needed social reforms. No doubt the belief that God himself through his Messiah would soon establish his kingdom and bring all men under his righteous judgment often had a conservative effect on the attitude of Christians toward the injustices of the world. Since the time was short, the believer could endure the wrongs inflicted on him with courage, looking forward to the new age when suffering and death would be no more. Yet Christians were constantly reminded that they too must stand before the divine judgment seat. (Romans 14:10; II Corinthians 5:10) There the test of the individual and of the community would be the treatment each had accorded to the least of the brethren of the Son of man. Wherever and whenever the church and its members have honestly tried to meet this exacting standard, the Christian "revolution" has gone forward. Meanwhile those who had submitted their lives to the lordship of Jesus were often hailed before the judgment seat of human authorities to give an account of the hope that was in them.

The Decrees of Caesar

Two stories in the book of Acts focus attention on the double obstacle which the church confronted in its mission to the world, the stories of Paul's work at Philippi and at Thessalonica. (Acts 16:11-17:9) Philippi was a military colony whose citizens enjoyed all the privileges of Roman law. However, some Jews residing there had established a "place of prayer" outside the gates of the city, where Paul spoke to a gathering of women. This suggests that there were not even enough male Jews in Philippi to organize a regular synagogue. At least, Luke described Paul's most prominent convert among these women, Lydia of Thyatira, as "a worshipper of God." This term was applied to Gentiles who were attached to the Jewish faith without becoming proselytes.

Soon Paul's activities at Philippi brought him into trouble with a group of soothsayers who took him before the magistrates of the city. The complaint alleged against him and Silas was: "These men are Jews and they are disturbing our city. They advocate customs which it is not lawful for us Romans to accept." Under Roman law, Judaism was a legal religion for Jews, but not for Roman citizens (who were obligated to observe the religion of the state). As long as Christianity remained a Jewish sect, there was no outside objection to its spread among the Jews themselves or to its making converts among non-citizens, but that was as far as it could go. So the apostles spent the night in jail, and it was then that Paul asserted his own rights as a Roman citizen, gaining an apology but not the privilege of preaching his faith without restriction.

At Thessalonica the opposition to Paul followed a somewhat different pattern. There was a Jewish synagogue in that city which Paul attended. Taking his texts from the Hebrew scriptures, he explained how the sufferings and resurrection of the Messiah had been prophesied, and said: "This Jesus, whom I proclaim to you, is the Christ." Here again, Paul's hearers included "devout Greeks" as well as leading women of the community, some of whom were persuaded by his words and joined him and Silas as believers. But the claim that Jesus was the Messiah was interpreted by some of the Jews in a political sense, just as it had been by the Jerusalem priesthood and by Pilate. So there was another public disturbance, and some of the brethren were dragged before the local magistrates.

The accusation against the apostles was more serious this time. They were accused of having "turned the world upside down," and of "acting against the decrees of Caesar, saying that there is another king, Jesus." This was the same thing as saying that Christians were a subversive element among the people, a revolutionary party like the Palestinian "Zealots." If Paul had been allowed his day in court at Thessalonica, perhaps he would have replied that it was not faith in Jesus that upset the world, for the world was already topsy-turvy through man's sinful rebellion against God's sovereignty and needed Christ to set it right. But on this occasion, Luke reported that the brethren sent Paul and Barnabas away by night to the neighboring town of Beroea, and for a while they were able to continue their mission in other cities, though seldom without meeting opposition.

Years later, standing before Festus, the Roman governor of Syria, and facing further serious charges made by Jewish opponents from Jerusalem, Paul made an appeal as a citizen to have his case transferred from the jurisdiction of the provincial court at Caesarea to that of Caesar's tribunal at Rome. This appeal was granted, and Paul's voyage to the imperial capital began. It was a journey he had long desired to make, but he had often been hindered by his determination to preach the gospel only where Christ was still unknown. So he had written his letter to the Roman Christians, telling them that as soon as he finished his work in the East he hoped to visit them on his way to Spain. (Romans 15:22-29) Whether Paul was ever permitted to carry on his proposed mission in lands that far to the West is a matter Luke failed to record, as he did also the circumstances of Paul's death. The fourth-century church historian Eusebius tried to make up this deficiency, but the evidence on which he had to rely was very scanty and uncertain. He believed that after trial at Rome Paul was released from prison, only to be rearrested later to stand a second trial at which he was condemned. All this he based on a letter believed to have been written by Paul, in which he mentioned "my first defense" and said, "I was rescued from the lion's mouth." (II Timothy 4:16-17) But most modern scholars are convinced on the basis of the Greek style of this letter that it was not actually written by Paul.

In spite of such uncertainty, there is little reason to doubt the tradition that Paul suffered martyrdom at the time of Nero's persecution of the Christians at Rome. In the face of that event, Paul's words to the Roman church with reference to the governing authorities of the empire seem rather ironical. "Would you have no fear of him who is in authority? Then do what is good, and you will receive his approval, for he is God's servant for your good." (Romans 13:2-4) That was no doubt an ideal of government as it should have been, but in first-century Rome, as in many other times and places, the ideal had been corrupted by a succession of selfish and cruel tyrants of whom Nero was perhaps the worst, but not the last. So the sword, which Paul had said the man in authority carried to execute punishment on the wrongdoer, was used to behead the apostle of Christ. Yet as a later defender of the faith was to say, "the blood of the martyrs is the seed of the church."

The Blood of the Martyrs

At least three books of the New Testament, and it is difficult to tell what others, were written largely in answer to the persecutions which the church suffered from the imperial government. These three books were the Gospel according to Mark, the First Epistle of Peter, and the Revelation to John. Perhaps, as we have already suggested, Luke's two volumes to Theophilus were also composed under similar circumstances, but this is uncertain. In other books, too, persecution is occasionally mentioned or hinted as a possible threat to the church.

In his church history Eusebius quoted a statement made by Irenaeus, bishop of Lyons in southern Gaul about A.D. 180, that Mark wrote his gospel "after the departure" of Peter and Paul. This is generally understood to mean that the earliest attempt to record the message preached by the apostles was made after their death—which would be most natural. So long as the original witnesses to Christ were alive, the church relied on their spoken testimony. But when persecution and martyrdom deprived the Christian community of their leadership, it seemed necessary to set down in written form all that could be remembered concerning the things said and done by Christ.

According to Mark, Jesus himself had foreseen that his followers would suffer "persecution on account of the word." (Mark 4:17; 10:30) Anticipating his own death, he had also said, "If any man would come after me, let him deny himself and take up his cross, and follow me." (Mark 8:34) In Eusebius' day it was reported that Peter had been crucified under Nero. Moreover, in veiled language about sharing his own baptism and drinking the cup he was to drink, Jesus had warned James and John that they must be prepared for martyrdom. Yet he had promised the disciples that when they were brought to trial before governors and kings for his sake, the Holy Spirit would inspire them to give true testimony, and "he who endures to the end will be saved." (Mark 13:9-13) With memories and assurances such as these, the church and its members were encouraged to continue to preach the gospel to all nations.

Until modern times it was generally supposed that the book known as the First Epistle of Peter was written by the apostle himself during the time of Nero's persecution at Rome. Today many scholars believe that the conditions faced by the Christians of Asia Minor, as this letter described them, were substantially the same as those which existed there during the reign of the emperor Trajan about fifty years later. Nero's persecution seems to have been directed only against Christians residing in the capital city, and did not extend to the provinces mentioned at the beginning of this letter. (I Peter 1:1) One of these provinces was Bithynia, where action against Christians was reported in a letter written, about A.D. 112, by the local governor, Pliny, and addressed to Trajan.

The problem which Pliny wished the emperor to settle was whether people should be punished simply for professing the name of Christian, or only for specific crimes proved against them. The writer of our New Testament letter attributed to Peter was concerned with the same problem. He told his readers that if they were reproached for the name of Christ, they were blessed. But none of them should suffer as a murderer, a thief, or for other crimes unworthy of a disciple. "Yet if one suffers as a Christian, let him not be ashamed, but under that name let him glorify God." (I Peter 4:14-16)

Pliny reported to Trajan a test to which he had subjected those who were accused of being Christians. He made them repeat after him an invocation to the Roman gods, and offer wine and incense before the emperor's statue. Those who refused were punished. In contrast to this, the New Testament writer advised his Christian readers to submit to the emperor and his governors in matters of law observance. But then he added, "Honor all men.

Love the brotherhood. Fear God. Honor the emperor." (I Peter 2:13-17) In other words, the emperor could be given as much respect as was fitting for "all men," but no more. Religious "fear" or reverence must be given to God only.

To encourage the persecuted brethren of Asia Minor to endure their unjust sufferings with patience, this author held before their eyes the example of Christ himself, who, when he was reviled, did not revile in return and when he suffered did not threaten retaliation, but trusted in God, the righteous judge. (I Peter 2:19-23) Finally, he closed his letter with a curious message: "She who is at Babylon, who is likewise chosen, sends you greetings." (I Peter 5:13) Later church writers probably interpreted the name "Babylon" correctly as a kind of secret code word meaning the city of Rome, and the "chosen" one as the congregation of Christians there. But if the original readers of the epistle were expected to understand the words in that way, the writer must have thought they already possessed some key to the symbol. That key had been furnished by the Revelation to John, which was likewise sent to Christian churches in Asia Minor.

Irenaeus declared that this Revelation "was seen not long ago, but almost in our own generation, at the end of the reign of Domitian." That means about A.D. 95. Other records of persecution under this emperor are rather obscure. The biographers, Suetonius and Dio Cassius, reported that Domitian punished a number of persons at Rome on charges of "atheism," or neglect of the state deities, and for adopting Jewish ways without making an open profession of Judaism. Perhaps this last was a vague attempt to describe people who had become Christians, since the early church claimed to be the true Israel of God.

The Christian prophet who wrote the book called Revelation thought of the church in exactly that way. He bitterly condemned "those who say that they are Jews and are not, but are a synagogue of Satan," presumably meaning Jews who denied the true Messiah. (Revelation 2:9; 3:9) On the other hand, he represented the church as "the holy city, new Jerusalem, coming down out of heaven from God, prepared as a bride adorned for her husband," the Messiah. (Revelation 21:2) His book was packed with ideas and phrases taken from the Hebrew scriptures, especially the book of Daniel. His own thoughts were strongly influenced by Daniel's visions of the judgment passed against the great beastlike powers which had oppressed God's people, and of the kingdom given to the saints represented by one like a son of man. (Daniel 7)

The climax of the Revelation to John was a similar series of visions of judgment against the persecuting empire of the author's own day. (Revelation 12-19) Near its close he gave his readers the necessary clue to his meaning. He had pictured a woman sitting on a scarlet beast full of blasphemous names, a beast having seven heads and ten horns. This woman's mysterious name was "Babylon the great, mother of harlots and earth's abominations." And she was drunk with the blood of the saints and martyrs of Jesus. Then an angel explained the secret. The seven heads of the beast stood for seven hills on which the "woman" was seated. Since this woman bore the name of a great city, few readers of that time needed to be told that she represented Rome, the "mother city" of the empire. Yet she was called a "harlot" which was a common Old Testament term for people unfaithful to God, especially through the worship of false gods and idols.

Earlier the author had said that those who refused to worship the image of the beast were slain. This would readily be understood since Christians refused to offer incense to the image of the emperor and the heads and horns of the beast were said to symbolize a succession of rulers who made war against the Messiah, "the Lamb." As for the blasphemous names and claims of the beast, every believer of that time must have remembered with horror that Domitian demanded that he should be addressed as "our Lord and God." But in the end the Lamb will conquer the beast, "for he is Lord of lords and King of kings." (Revelation

17:14; 19:16) After this victory the saints and martyrs who had refused to worship the beast and had been beheaded for their testimony to Jesus were expected to rise from the dead and reign with Christ a thousand years.

With such hopes and dreams, drawn from the earlier messianic expectations of the Jews, John tried to encourage the Christian congregations of Asia Minor to maintain their faith and endurance in the face of suffering and danger. He pictured Christ as saying to them, "Be faithful unto death, and I will give you the crown of life." But although, like the First Epistle of Peter, the book of Revelation reminded persecuted Christians that Christ himself had endured suffering and death, its author failed to recall how Jesus had borne the injustice without threatening retaliation. The theme of his book, unlike other parts of the New Testament, was not the forgiveness and reconciliation of the world to God, but terrible judgment and punishment for the wicked and the unbelievers. For centuries doubt concerning the identity of the author kept the book from gaining an undisputed place in the New Testament collection, but by the end of the fourth century it was generally accepted. Perhaps its best claim to such acceptance was its author's unshakable conviction that ultimately the crucified Christ will overcome the world. It is a book full of faith and hope, but singularly lacking in that Christian charity which Paul called the greatest of all virtues.

Hope Deferred

The Revelation to John ended with a promise that the day of the Lord's triumph was near at hand as the prophet heard Christ announce, "Surely I am coming soon." Speaking for the persecuted church of his time, the author responded with a prayer of fervent hope and desire: "Amen. Come, Lord Jesus!" (Revelation 22:20) That same prayer had been uttered more than a generation earlier by Paul, who still repeated the Aramaic words of the earliest Jewish disciples, *Marana tha*, meaning "Our Lord, come!" (I Corinthians 16:22) It had been recorded that Jesus himself had said that some of his disciples would not experience death before they should see God's reign coming with power. (Mark 9:1)

As time passed and most of the original followers of Jesus died, a rumor continued to persist that at least one of them was to survive until his return. But the compiler of the latest gospel record took pains to correct that rumor as a misunderstanding of something Jesus had said to Peter about an unnamed disciple whom he loved. Jesus had never said that this man was not to die, but only "If it is my will that he remain until I come, what is that to you? Follow me!" (John 21:20-23) It was a warning to the church, such as Luke placed at the beginning of the book of Acts, that it was not for the disciples to know the times or seasons which the Father had fixed by his own authority. All that was required of them was to continue to be Christ's witnesses to the ends of the earth. (Acts 1:6-8) In fact Jesus himself had said that of the day or hour when the Son of man would come, no one knows, not even the angels in heaven nor the Son, but only the Father. (Mark 13:32)

This problem of hope long deferred was still making the heart of many sick when one of the latest books in the New Testament collection was written, about A.D. 150. The writer predicted that scoffers would say even in the last days, "Where is the promise of his coming? For ever since the fathers fell asleep, all things have continued as they were from the beginning of creation." To this the writer replied that the Lord had not been slow about keeping his promise but was simply showing patience with men, not wishing any to perish but that all should come to repentance. No one could tell just when the day of the Lord might arrive since it would come unexpectedly like a thief. Men must remember that in the Lord's sight one day is like a thousand years and a thousand years like one day. But that should not be taken to mean the world would go on forever, and believers should wait patiently for new heavens and a new earth in which righteousness will dwell. (II Peter 3:3-13)

Although that hope might lie far in the future, the church repeated and cherished the words of the Lord which gave assurance of his continuing presence among his people. Wherever even two or three might gather in his name, he would be there in the midst of them. Indeed, he will stay with them as long as this age shall last. (Matthew 18:20; 28:20) While the world would no longer see him, he would make his home with those who love him and keep his words. Through the Spirit of truth as their counsellor they would be helped to remember all that Jesus had taught them and be guided into all the truth. (John 14:15-27; 16:13) With such divine assurances the church could face the future with courage and confidence.

CHAPTER FIVE

FACING THE FUTURE

Jesus had given his disciples no clearly marked map to follow as they went out into the world to preach the gospel. He had drawn no blueprints for the new temple of the Spirit which they were to build. He had laid down no legal constitution for the government of the church, which was yet unborn when the authorities of Palestine tried to end his mission by putting him to death. What Jesus had done was to proclaim the reign of God over the lives of men and to choose, from among his hearers, a small company of close companions whom he trained to share his own mission.

Mark described this significant step in the ministry of Jesus, as he did most others, in bare outline. Later gospel writers attempted to fill in such details as might still be remembered, but the earliest account said only this:

> And he went up into the hills, and called to him those whom he desired; and they came to him. And he appointed twelve, to be with him, and to be sent out to preach and have authority to cast out demons. (Mark 3:13-15)

To this Mark was able to append a list of names, several of them already familiar to the readers of his gospel. There were the four fishermen whom Jesus had called to follow him as he went into Capernaum to begin his teaching: Simon and Andrew his brother, and James and John the two sons of Zebedee. There was also a man named James the son of Alphaeus. Mark's readers would remember that earlier they had read a story about Jesus inviting a man named Levi the son of Alphaeus to follow him. (Mark 2:13-15) This man was evidently a tax collector, one of the despised class of "publicans and sinners." But Mark failed to say whether Alphaeus had two sons, one named Levi, the other James, or whether the two names belonged to the same man. It is a question that remains unanswered.

The only other member of the original twelve about whom Mark had special information was Judas Iscariot, who later betrayed Jesus. But he knew nothing to report about Philip and Bartholomew, Matthew and Thomas, Thaddaeus and Simon the Cananaean. This second Simon in the list, called "the Cananaean" to distinguish him from Simon called Peter, was undoubtedly the man whom Luke called "the Zealot." (Luke 6:15; Acts 1:13) In one list, Matthew was called "the tax collector," and his name was then substituted for Levi in the story of his call. (Matthew 9:9; 10:3) The fourth and last of the gospel records included several stories about Philip and Thomas, as well as one about a man named Nathanael. But there was no indication that this man was one of the twelve, although some have supposed Nathanael to be another name for Bartholomew.

In the book of Acts, the mission of the twelve was to bear witness to Jesus and particularly to his resurrection. This was the purpose for which Matthias was chosen to take the place of the traitor Judas Iscariot. But in Luke's lists in the gospel and Acts, there was also another Judas, described simply as the son of James. Apparently nothing more was known about him. All this suggests that by the time the various gospel records were written there was uncertainty about the exact names of some of these twelve men, and of many of them only the names were remembered.

Two of the twelve were mentioned with some frequency in Acts, Peter and John, who seem at first to have worked together as a team. Later stories of Peter's activities pictured him working more or less alone. Since Herod Agrippa I was reported to have beheaded James, the brother of John, shortly before his own death in A.D. 44, it is possible that other members of the twelve were also slain at an early date, including John as well. At any rate, Mark knew of a saying of Jesus in which he was believed to have predicted the martyrdom of both James and John. (Mark 10:39) Peter too had been arrested by Herod and had narrowly escaped with his life. (Acts 12:1-17)

One by one, the apostolic missionaries departed; Peter and Paul, it was generally believed, in the persecution of Nero in A.D. 64. The apostles' limited historical outlook had not permitted them to foresee that the church was to continue in the world for centuries after their time. They expected all institutions of this world to pass away, giving place to the eternal reality of God's reign. In the holy city, new Jerusalem, there would be no need even for a temple, for God himself would be its sanctuary. (Revelation 21:22) The most that any of the earliest Christian writers, like Paul, felt called to do for the Christian communities to which they addressed their occasional messages was to deal with the practical problems immediately facing them. The advice which Paul gave to a particular local congregation was not intended to settle matters for every congregation everywhere, nor for all time.

Although Paul felt it necessary to make a distinction between instructions received from the Lord, and others in which he could only give his own personal opinion, he concluded such advice by saying, "I think that I have the Spirit of God." (I Corinthians 7:40) One could wish that leaders of the church in all ages had shown as much humility, making no impossible claim to infallible judgment or a monopoly on divine truth. All that the Lord had promised was that the Spirit of truth would continue to guide his disciples as new and different problems arose. He never said that every problem would be settled for them in advance, or that the order followed in the past was to become an immutable law governing the present and the future.

Thus the New Testament has preserved a picture of the church as a living, growing organism, constantly undergoing changes in thought and structure, during the century between A.D. 50 and 150, in which these twenty-seven books were written.

New Occasions, New Duties

Growth always brings about changes in an organism, and the rapid growth of the early church likewise produced many changes in its life and activities. So far as the Christian community could be thought of as a body, changes affecting it were often of the kind readily perceptible to the physical eye or ear. For example, descriptions of the assembly for worship given by later church writers of the second and third centuries present quite different pictures from the one drawn by Paul in his first letter to the Corinthians.

In Paul's time there seems to have been no fixed day for such meetings, for he knew of Christians who esteemed all days alike, as well as others who observed a particular day in honor of the Lord. To Paul it apparently made no difference. (Romans 14: 5-6) His request to the Corinthians, that each of them should put aside some contribution for the poor "on the first day of the week" in no way indicates that the congregation actually met on that day. On the contrary, these offerings were to be stored up at home until Paul returned to Corinth. (I Corinthians 16:1-2) In contrast to this, Luke reported a gathering of Christians on the first day of the week at Troas, which included a suppertime breaking of bread, after which Paul continued to speak to the congregation until midnight. (Acts 20:7) Beyond this one incident there is no record in the New Testament, except the obscure statement of the prophet John: "I was in the Spirit on the Lord's day." (Revelation 1:10) Probably the churches of Asia to which he wrote understood which day of the week he meant, since he did not think it necessary to explain. It was Justin, who died as a martyr at Rome about A.D. 165, who recorded that by

that time Christians were accustomed to hold their common assembly on Sunday, the day on which God began creation and on
which Jesus Christ the Savior rose from the dead.

The directions Paul gave to the Corinthian congregation, about
keeping their enthusiasm in bounds lest it create confusion in
their meeting, were necessary just because there was no chairman
with authority to maintain order, and every member was free to
speak as the Spirit moved him. When Justin wrote in the latter
half of the second century, there was a "president of the brethren" who offered prayers and thanksgivings to the Father through
the name of his Son and of the Holy Spirit; and to this the people all said *Amen*, a Hebrew word already in use in Paul's day.
Justin explained that this word meant "may it come to pass." He
also mentioned regular readings from "the memoirs of the apostles" called gospels, or from the writings of the prophets.

If the meetings of Paul's time included any reading from the
scriptures, he failed to mention it. Certainly none of the gospel
records existed in written form that early. Instead, the gospel
was something to be "preached" by word of mouth. In Paul's absence, there might be a letter from him to be read to the congregation. But no one, least of all Paul himself, thought of these letters as "scriptures" in the same sense that the term was applied
to the law and the prophets. At most, the reading of the epistle
took the place of a "sermon" which the apostle might have delivered in person if he had been present. Occasionally, two
neighboring congregations might exchange letters each had received from Paul, as he had directed to be done on one occasion.
(Colossians 4:16) Eventually, years after Paul's death, some
one undertook to collect all his letters which still survived. By
the time one of the last books of the New Testament was written,
about A.D. 150, its author put Paul's collected letters in the same
class with "the other scriptures." (II Peter 3:15-16)

Such changes in the practice of the early church were often
more noticeable than others which may have affected its thought

and life even more deeply. As a person grows, changes taking place in his appearance or in the structure of his body are usually more evident than those subtle changes of thought and mind which invariably accompany such growth. So with the growth of the church. Its central faith and message, the gospel of Jesus Christ, was to remain constant because he is the same yesterday and today and forever. Yet different teachers interpreted that message in different terms, at various times and places. Thus the problem soon arose whether every new interpretation of the church's faith could be accepted as true, or whether certain attempts to expound it must be rejected as false. This in turn raised further questions, by what standards Christian truth could be distinguished from falsehood and who should decide between them.

The first test of truth acknowledged by the church was the word of the Lord. As that word had been spoken in the past by inspired prophets and teachers, it had been handed down in the holy scriptures, the books of the "old covenant." Those scriptures had been interpreted and "fulfilled" by Christ himself. Through him God had poured out the Holy Spirit on the earliest disciples, who spoke in Christ's name. In Christian assemblies the same Spirit had continued to give the utterance of wisdom and knowledge to apostles, prophets, and teachers, and to bestow on others gifts of healing as well as of "tongues." Under the guidance of the Spirit, Paul had written his letters to the churches. But a later writer, while admitting the wisdom contained in those letters complained, "There are some things in them hard to understand, which the ignorant and unstable twist to their own destruction, as they do the other scriptures." (II Peter 3:16)

Soon there was a growing collection of scriptures belonging to the new covenant, or New Testament. Chief among these were the four gospel records. By the end of the second century it was generally believed that two of these four books had been written by the apostles Matthew and John. The other two also might claim "apostolic" authority, since Mark was said to have been Peter's interpreter, while Luke had been a companion of Paul. In fact, Irenaeus of Lyons argued that it was impossible for the gospel collection to include either fewer or more than just these four books. Although Irenaeus did not mention any others by name, two decades later Clement of Alexandria knew and quoted a gospel "according to the Hebrews" and one "according to the Egyptians." Soon there were a number of apocryphal gospels, some containing doctrines which the church found it necessary to reject as utterly false and dangerous.

One of these apocryphal gospels, falsely attributed to the apostle Thomas, was recovered rather recently in Egypt as part of a manuscript written in a Coptic dialect, probably in the fifth century. However, fragments of its text in the original Greek had been known to scholars for more than half a century through other papyrus manuscripts, likewise discovered in Egypt. Although this so-called Gospel according to Thomas claims to preserve "the secret words of Jesus," more than half its contents repeat in slightly different form parables, like that of the sower, and other sayings already familiar to every reader of the New Testament. On the other hand, in one episode Jesus is said to have taken Thomas aside privately and spoken to him three words. When his fellow-disciples asked him what the Master had said, Thomas replied, "If I were to tell you one of the words which he said to me, you would take up stones and cast them at me, and fire would come out of the stones and consume you." In the face of such risks, it is scarcely surprising that the reader likewise never learns what these secret words were alleged to have been! Since death by stoning was the Jewish punishment for uttering the divine name, some scholars have hazarded the guess that the three words may have some reference to the Trinity. However, that is not very likely, since the Father, the Son and the Holy Spirit are mentioned together quite openly in another part of this document.

Even some teachers who claimed to base their doctrines on the accepted scriptures "twisted" the texts they quoted in order to support fanciful meanings of their own invention. Occasionally, such men laid claim to special gifts of wisdom and knowledge, either by direct inspiration or by means of secret traditions unknown to other church leaders, which contradicted the scriptures themselves. This led one writer to assert that "no prophecy of scripture is a matter of one's own interpretation" and to warn his readers against false teachers who "secretly bring in destructive heresies, even denying the Master who bought them." (II Peter 1:20; 2:1) In the face of this internal crisis the church began to formulate additional standards by which the truth could be distinguished from falsehood. It also invested certain tried and proven leaders with the authority of applying these standards as a test of the doctrines taught by any new teacher. Thus the church's struggle against false doctrine or heresy contributed directly to the making of a creed, and to the development of an ordained ministry.

One God, One Lord, One Spirit

When Jesus had preached "the kingdom of God," he had taught no new doctrine, but only the faith which Judaism had inherited from the great insight of the prophets, that Israel's God is "Lord of heaven and earth." (Matthew 11:25; Luke 10:21) No matter how much different sects of Jews might disagree on other points, one article of faith was common to them all. There is no other deity beside the one true God, the sovereign creator of the world and of all races of men who dwell in it. This central truth, concerning the unity and uniqueness of God, was affirmed in the synagogue by the recitation of a passage of scripture, beginning with the familiar words:

Hear, O Israel: The Lord our God is one Lord; and you shall love
the Lord your God with all your heart, and with all your soul, and
with all your might. (Deuteronomy 6:4-6)

This was the nearest approach to a creed that could be found in
Judaism. It was said that when a man confessed the truth of
these words, he accepted "the yoke of the sovereignty of heaven."
That is, he acknowledged God as the only Lord and King of his
life. Jesus repeated these words when one of the scribes asked
him which was the first commandment of all. (Mark 12:28-30)

When the earliest followers of Jesus went out to preach the gospel to the world, they maintained this monotheistic faith of all
devout Jews. Among educated Greeks and Romans there were
already some who had begun to approach a similar faith. Many
took the view that people of different races and nations merely
used different names for the same deity or deities, and in any
case there was one god who reigned supreme over all the others.
But the great masses of people were usually quite ready to accept
some new or strange deity in addition to the many gods and lords
they already worshipped. So it was always necessary for Christian teachers to make clear to their Gentile converts that the
Lord Jesus whom they proclaimed was not just one lord among
many.

In a letter to Christians at Corinth, Paul thought it important
to remind them that "for us there is one God, the Father," going
on at once to add "and one Lord, Jesus Christ." (I Corinthians
8:5-6) Writing to the church at Thessalonica, he recalled how
they had "turned to God from idols, to serve a living and true
God, and to wait for his Son from heaven, whom he raised from
the dead, Jesus who delivers us from the wrath to come." (I
Thessalonians 1:9-10) It was God himself who bestowed on Jesus
"the name which is above every name." Therefore, every one
who confesses that Jesus Christ is "Lord" gives glory to God the
Father. (Philippians 2:9-11) The twofold faith of the early
Christians was already approaching credal form when Paul wrote:

"If you confess with your lips that Jesus is Lord and believe in your heart that God raised him from the dead, you will be saved." (Romans 10:9)

It was "in the name of Jesus Christ," or of "the Lord Jesus," that converts to this faith were baptized. (Acts 2:38; 8:16; 10:48; 19:5) Paul spoke of people being "baptized into Christ Jesus," and also of being baptized "in one Spirit." (Romans 6:3; I Corinthians 12:13) In fact, he said no one could call Jesus "Lord," except by the Holy Spirit, who also enabled believers to call God "Father." (I Corinthians 12:3; Romans 8:15; Galatians 4:6) So as time went on, it must have seemed appropriate that converts should be baptized "in the name of the Father and of the Son and of the Holy Spirit." It was even said that the risen Lord himself had commanded the use of these words. (Matthew 28:19)

This baptismal formula in the name of the Trinity was gradually expanded into a "rule of faith" which could be taught to new converts as a safeguard against false doctrines. Toward the end of the second century Irenaeus of Lyons summarized the faith taught by the apostles in statements closely resembling those later contained in the "Apostles' Creed." Practically every article in that creed was denied by some false teacher or other during the period when it was being drawn up. Thus the church tried to overcome error by affirming what it believed to be the word of truth.

This method of meeting false ideas with positive statements of truth had been used by Paul. After the Colossian Christians had been converted by the preaching of one of his younger helpers, a man named Epaphras, this man visited Paul to get his advice about a serious problem. The faith of the Colossians was in danger of being corrupted by a curious mixture of the gospel with ideas which were largely pagan, and even polytheistic. Someone in the congregation was teaching a "philosophy" which pictured the universe as under the control of a number of "elemental spirits" called "thrones, dominions, principalities, authorities." This teacher insisted that such spirits or "angels" should be worshipped as deities. He evidently believed that the material world and man's physical body are evil, for he had persuaded the Colossians to submit to ascetic regulations: "Do not handle, Do not taste, Do not touch." (Colossians 2:8-21)

Paul's letter to the Colossians gave his answer to this false version of Christianity. He began by asserting the supremacy of Christ over all created beings, both in heaven and on earth, visible and invisible. This meant that he is Lord even over those "angels" which the false teacher said should be worshipped. Perhaps this teacher had even denied that Christ had a "body of flesh," for Paul affirmed this fact, adding "in him the whole fulness of the deity dwells bodily." As for ascetic rules, Paul denied they were of any moral value since Christian virtues grow from the inner life of the Spirit. (Colossians 1:15-20; 2:9; 2:23; 3:17)

False ideas of this kind continued to disturb the churches of Asia Minor and other regions for several generations. Toward the beginning of the second century, the author of two New Testament books denounced as deceivers those who would not acknowledge the coming of Jesus Christ in the flesh. (I John 4:2-3; II John 7) This meant the refusal to admit that Jesus had ever lived as man among men, hungry and in need of food, subject to suffering and death. At most, he had merely "appeared" to have a human body and to die on the cross, but he had not really done so. From a Greek word meaning "to appear" or "seem," those who taught this strange doctrine came to be known as Docetists, while their heresy was called Docetism.

One of the chief opponents of Docetism was Ignatius, bishop of Antioch until his martyrdom under Trajan, about A.D. 117. Writing to various churches in Asia Minor, he warned Christians not to fall into the snare of this false doctrine, but to be fully convinced of the birth and the suffering and death of Jesus Christ, which latter actually took place when Pontius Pilate was procurator. In other words, Ignatius affirmed that Christ was a real historical person, not a phantom, not a mythological character like the gods and heroes of the heathen. Thus Ignatius urged the readers of his letter to the church at Tralles:

> Turn a deaf ear when any one speaks to you contrary to Jesus Christ. He was of the family of David, and of Mary. He was really born. He ate and drank. He was really persecuted under Pontius Pilate. He was really crucified and died, while creatures in heaven, on earth and under the earth looked on. He was really raised from the dead, his Father having raised him up.

He added that God will raise up those who believe in Christ, apart from whom we have no real life.

All this looks very much like the beginnings of a creed, which asserts in positive form everything the Docetists denied. While the language varied from letter to letter, the main points were usually the same. For example, in the letter to Smyrna, after glorifying Christ as God, he says:

> He is really of the family of David according to the flesh, Son of God according to the will and power of God, really born of a virgin, baptized by John in order that all righteousness might be fulfilled by him, really nailed in flesh for us under Pontius Pilate and Herod the tetrarch.

Further on he asserted, "I know and believe that even after the resurrection he was in flesh." It is probable from this passage that Ignatius was familiar with a number of statements about Christ in the New Testament. (Romans 1:3-4; Matthew 3:15; perhaps Luke 24:39) Consequently, although he never quotes either of the two stories about the birth of Jesus which have so deeply influenced our celebration of Christmas, he may have known at least one of them.

The earliest of the gospel records, the one composed by Mark, concentrated its attention entirely on the brief public ministry of Jesus. It made no mention of his birth, or of any other event in his life before his baptism in the river Jordan. As he came up out of its waters, the Spirit descended upon him, and he heard a voice from heaven, saying, "Thou art my beloved Son; in thee I am well pleased." Two of the later evangelists repeated this story much as Mark told it, though a few ancient texts of Luke 3:22 have an exact quotation of Psalm 2:7, "Thou art my Son; today I have begotten thee." These words were evidently a favorite messianic proof text among early Christians, who applied them to Jesus. (Acts 13:33; Hebrews 1:5; 5:5) Moreover, in two of the gospels, the story of the crucifixion reached its climax in the confession of the Roman centurion, "Truly this man was a son of God." (Matthew 27:54; Mark 15:39)

Unfortunately converts from various pagan religions of the time could interpret such statements in accord with their former beliefs. They were familiar with Greek myths about heroes who were deified after death, as well as with a Roman custom of calling the emperor "a son of God." Thus it was possible for such people to think of the Lord Jesus as a man who had become divine. Some of them may have supposed that this happened when the Spirit of God came upon him at his baptism. Others might have thought that it occurred when he rose victorious over death. It is even possible that some Roman Christians thought that was what Paul meant when he wrote at the beginning of his letter to them:

> Who was descended from David according to the flesh, and designated Son of God in power according to the Spirit of holiness by his resurrection from the dead, Jesus Christ our Lord. (Romans 1:3-4)

But to any one familiar with other letters of Paul it is clear that this was not at all what he believed or taught.

On the contrary, Paul thought of Christ's years on earth as a temporary episode in the life of an eternal being who came from a different realm. Thus he affirmed that "when the time had fully come, God sent forth his Son," to be born of a woman, under the law. (Galatians 4:4) Or again, "though he was in the form of God, [Christ] did not count equality with God a thing to be grasped, but emptied himself, taking the form of a servant, being born in the likeness of men." (Philippians 2:6-7) More than that, "he is the image of the invisible God, the first born of all creation; for in him all things were created . . . He is before all things, and in him all things hold together." (Colossians 1:15-17) Yet Paul nowhere attempted to answer the question, how the Son of God had become man. It was enough to believe that in him all the fullness of God was pleased to dwell, so that believers come to fullness of life in him. (Colossians 1:19; 2:9)

A generation later, Luke began his gospel with the now familiar story of an angelic announcement made to Mary, the mother of Jesus, when she was betrothed, but not yet married to Joseph. "The Holy Spirit will come upon you, and the power of the Most High will overshadow you; therefore the child to be born will be called holy, the Son of God." (Luke 1:35) The Gospel according to Matthew, written about the same time or shortly afterward, reported a similar revelation to Joseph. "Do not fear to take Mary your wife, for that which is conceived in her is of the Holy Spirit; she will bear a son, and you shall call his name Jesus, for he will save his people from their sins." (Matthew 1:20-21) To this the evangelist added his own comment:

> All this took place to fulfill what the Lord had spoken by the prophet: 'Behold, a virgin shall conceive and bear a son, and his name shall be called Emmanuel' (which means, God with us). (Matthew 1:22-23)

The words quoted by the gospel writer were taken directly from the Greek version of the Septuagint.

Jewish opponents were quick to point out that the original words of the prophet made no reference to a virgin. Literally translated, they stated simply that "a young woman shall conceive and bear a son." (Isaiah 7:14) Jews had read these words for centuries without finding anything extraordinary in them. In answer to such objections, defenders of the faith, like Justin the martyr, who sincerely believed that the Septuagint preserved the true meaning of the prophecy, accused Jewish scribes of altering the Hebrew text. Although no evidence of such alteration has ever been discovered, as long as the earliest Hebrew manuscripts available came from the ninth and tenth centuries of the Christian era, such suspicions were still possible. The Dead Sea Scrolls have brought to light a complete text of Isaiah, which most competent scholars recognize as having been penned before the time of Christ. In Chapter 7:14, this scroll reads: "a young woman shall conceive and bear a son." We may be reasonably sure that these were the original words of the prophet.

Thus the value of these stories concerning the birth of Jesus must lie elsewhere than in the belief that they are the literal fulfillment of an ancient prophecy. Near the beginning of the fifth century, Augustine of Hippo interpreted these narratives as evidence that a miraculous conception and birth, without a human father, was necessary to preserve Jesus from an inherited tendency to sin, said to be transmitted through the natural union of man and woman. Since careful reading of the gospel stories themselves reveals no hint of such an idea, we cannot suppose this to have been the belief which the evangelists intended to teach. What these writers did believe is clear enough. They were convinced that the coming of Jesus Christ was a mighty act of God. It was the work of the Holy Spirit, the power of the Most High. Jesus is truly Son of God, just as he is truly man.

All the gospel writers, including Mark, proclaimed that Jesus is Son of God, the one who has the power of the Spirit. The apostles had preached that faith long before any such stories were put into written form. On this point there was real unity of conviction and teaching among the earliest Christians in spite of the variety of its expression. Yet the stories of the birth of

Jesus left unanswered the important question whether Christ first came into existence when his mother conceived by the Holy Spirit. Neither Matthew nor Luke specifically stated that Christ is the eternal being, by whom the entire universe was created. The clearest statements of this conviction are made by Paul, followed by the later writers of the Epistle to the Hebrews and of the fourth gospel, that according to John.

This gospel was probably published at Ephesus about the time of the Docetist controversy. The evangelist may also have been the writer of the two letters which condemned as deceivers those who denied that Christ came in the flesh. (I John 4:2-3; II John 7) In the second of these he called himself "the elder," without mentioning his name, though presumably the recipients of the letter knew who he was. What concerns us here is not his identity, but his doctrine. Like Mark, this evangelist said nothing about the birth of Christ, for like Paul he believed that the work of Christ had not begun with his coming to earth. So he opened his book with the well-known lines which take us back to the Old Testament story of creation:

> In the beginning was the Word, and the Word was with God, and the Word was God. He was in the beginning with God; all things were made through him, and without him was not anything made that was made. (John 1:1-3)

So in line after line of the poetic hymn which followed, he asserted the faith Paul had preached in earlier days. All things were created through Christ. He is the true light that enlightens every man. He has given believers power to become children of God. (Colossians 1:16; I Corinthians 8:6; II Corinthians 4:5-6; Galatians 3:26; 4:6) Docetists might have agreed with such statements, although they would have protested that the material world is evil and could not have been made by Christ.

The climax of this poem was the affirmation: "The Word became flesh and dwelt among us, full of grace and truth." (John

1:14) Here was the fact which Docetists denied. If any of them bothered to read further, they soon found other statements which flatly contradicted their own peculiar doctrines. There was a story, not included in the earlier records, about Jesus sitting down to rest beside a well and asking a woman who came to draw water to give him a drink. Surely this was a real human person who became wearied with his journey, and no mere phantom. If the reader persisted to the end, he would learn that Jesus had wept at the tomb of Lazarus his friend, and that on the cross he had cried out, "I thirst." After he died, a soldier pierced his side with a spear, causing blood and water to flow from the wound. No such details were mentioned in the earlier records, but the latest gospel writer considered them important, probably because they served to demonstrate the reality of Christ's suffering and death. The eternal Son of God had not come "disguised" as a man; he was truly man.

Among other New Testament books written in opposition to false doctrines were the three known as the "pastoral epistles": First and Second Timothy, and Titus. In the first of these, the writer called the church "the pillar and bulwark of truth" and then went on to confess what he called "the mystery of our religion." This was contained in a brief, easily memorized series of statements about Christ:

> He was manifested in the flesh,
> vindicated in the Spirit,
> seen by angels,
> preached among the nations,
> believed on in the world,
> taken up in glory. (I Timothy 3:16)

It began with a reference to the real humanity of Christ, and went on to speak of his recognition by angels in heaven, as well as by men on earth who came to believe in him through the preaching of the gospel.

Like the false doctrine at Colossae, the one combatted in this letter included ideas from pagan "philosophy," for the author closed with the warning: "Avoid godless chatter and contradictions of what is falsely called knowledge, for by professing it some have missed the mark as regards the faith." (I Timothy 6:20-21) Because they claimed they had received some divine revelation of "knowledge," for which the Greek term was *gnosis*, certain pseudo-philosophers at that time were dubbed Gnostics. This name was often used by church writers of the second and third centuries to describe their heretical opponents. Irenaeus of Lyons called his long work against heresies "A Refutation and Overthrow of What Is Falsely Called Knowledge."

One of the teachers attacked by Irenaeus was a man named Marcion, a native of Pontus in northern Asia Minor, where his father was said to have been a bishop of the church at Sinope. Some time before A.D. 140, Marcion traveled to Rome, where he began to teach doctrines which he claimed were the true version of the gospel preached by Paul. He also wrote a book which he called "Contradictions," designed to prove that the gospel of Christ is so contrary to the Hebrew scriptures that the same God could not have inspired both. For example, the law had said, "Cursed be every one who hangs on a tree"; but Paul said, "Christ redeemed us from the curse of the law." (Galatians 3:13) To Marcion this meant that the God of the law had actually cursed Christ. That God was also said to be the creator of the world which is evil, and he was therefore an inferior being, who held men as his slaves through fear of the law's curse. But at last, "the unknown God," who is loving and merciful, sent his Son to deliver men from the God of the law. Like the false teaching at Colassae, Marcion's system seems to have included a set of ascetic rules, for he was said to despise the flesh and to forbid marriage.

Many statements made by the author of the pastoral epistles affirm the points which Marcion denied: "We know that the law is good" and "there is one God, and there is one mediator between God and men, the man Christ Jesus, who gave himself as a ransom for all." (I Timothy 1:8; 2:5) In harmony with the Hebrew scriptures, he asserted: "Everything created by God is good, and nothing is to be rejected if it is received with thanksgiving." (I Timothy 4:4) This comes immediately after a warning against those who depart from the faith, forbidding marriage and demanding abstinence from foods which God created to be received with thanksgiving by those who know and believe the truth. (I Timothy 4:1-3) The other epistles in this group contain similar warnings against false doctrines, and there is the statement: "All scripture is inspired by God." (II Timothy 3:16) This would include the law and the prophets as well as the gospel and the letters of Paul. Readers were urged to avoid dissensions and quarrels about the law. As for a factious man, after one or two admonitions, Christians should have no more to do with him, as a perverted and sinful person who is self-condemned. (Titus 3:10) This was the actual fate of Marcion, who was expelled from the Roman congregation as a "heretic," a Greek term meaning "factious."

It was against men like Marcion, men who departed so far from the original faith of the church that they could believe in the existence of two deities, the lesser of whom created the world, that the Apostles' Creed began with the affirmation: "I believe in God, the Father Almighty, Maker of heaven and earth." Yet Marcion's movement was not silenced at once, for he organized a church of his own and was reported to have made converts from every race of men. In the face of such powerful opposition, the church made new efforts to strengthen its own organization, that it might more effectively combat error and carry the truth of the gospel to all nations.

Guarding the Truth

The chief "ministers" of the church in its earliest days were
known as apostles, prophets, and teachers. On this point, the
first hand reports of Paul corroborate the records given later by
Luke in the book of Acts.

At Jerusalem, the term "apostle" was used chiefly to designate
a member of the group of twelve men chosen and sent out by
Jesus to extend his own mission of preaching the reign of God.
It is uncertain, in fact doubtful, whether Jesus himself ever used
this term, or any Aramaic word corresponding to it. For in
the earliest gospel record the Greek term was used only once,
but not in a quotation of any words of Jesus, where Mark reported the return of "the apostles" from their mission. There it
meant simply "the messengers," those whom Jesus had sent out
two by two. (Mark 6:7, 30) Similarly, in the Gospel according
to Matthew there is a single occurrence of the term at the beginning of the list of names of "the twelve apostles." (Matthew
10:2) Luke alone used the term more frequently in his gospel,
as well as in the Acts, and he alone claimed that when Jesus
chose the twelve he named them "apostles." (Luke 6:13)

Modern scholars have devoted much study to a Hebrew word
used among the Jews to describe a messenger who was given authority to represent the person or group of persons by whom
he was sent. This Hebrew word *shaliach* could be represented
in Greek by the term *apostolos*. On the basis of such studies it
is sometimes said that Jesus commissioned the twelve to be his
personal delegates, with legal authority to act in his name.
Those who interpret the mission of the twelve in this way point
to his words: "He who receives you receives me, and he who receives me receives him who sent me." (Matthew 10:40)

Further study of the use of the term *shaliach* in Judaism reveals several significant points often overlooked in discussions

of the work of Christian apostles. First, such "delegates" were
sent on missions of limited duration. They were authorized to
represent the sender only in places and in relation to people he
could not visit in person. When they returned and reported the
successful completion of their errand, their commission ended,
although it might later be renewed for some other task. Second,
if anything like sickness or approaching death prevented the
delegate from completing his task, he had no authority to commission someone else to take his place. Finally, official "delegates" of the Jewish religious community, although sent out to
supervise the teaching of the synagogues in the Dispersion, did
not function as "missionaries" to the Gentiles. Christian "apostles," on the other hand, always served as "evangelists" for the
conversion of unbelievers.

Only a study of the New Testament records can reveal the
actual functions of the Christian apostles, and the work most
prominently mentioned there is that of "preaching the gospel."
Both in Paul's letters and in the Acts, an apostle is a "witness" to
Christ. He is one who has seen the risen Lord. (Acts 1:21-22;
2:32; 3:15; I Corinthians 9:1; 15:8-10) This evidently included
many others beside the twelve, since Paul reported that Jesus
had appeared to the twelve, and later "to all the apostles."
(I Corinthians 15:5, 7) Luke called both Barnabas and Paul
apostles. (Acts 14:14) Paul applied the term to Andronicus and
Junias, and perhaps to James the Lord's brother. (Romans 16:7;
Galatians 1:19) Epaphroditus was a "messenger" or apostle of
the congregation at Philippi. (Philippians 2:25)

None of the legalism which characterized the Jewish "delegate"
attached itself to the apostles in the New Testament. Their authority came from their testimony to the truth, an inward and
spiritual authority. It could not be delegated to others. This fact
was made clear by the story of an emergency which occurred
early in the growth of the community of disciples at Jerusalem.
Evidently a number of Hellenists, or Greek-speaking Jews, had

accepted the new faith. But in the daily distribution of food, their dependents, particularly widows, were neglected by the Aramaic-speaking congregation. So the twelve called a meeting of all the disciples and said: "It is not right that we should give up preaching the word of God to serve tables." What they proposed was this. The brethren were to seek out seven of their number who were "full of the Spirit and of wisdom" to be appointed to meet the need, while the twelve devoted themselves to prayer and "the ministry of the word." After choice had been made by the congregation, the seven were presented to the twelve, who prayed and laid their hands on them. (Acts 6:1-6)

This has often been called the "ordination" of the first "deacons." Although Luke did not use the Greek noun from which our English word "deacon" was derived, that term originally meant a household "servant" whose duties included waiting on tables. The seven men elected by the congregation of the disciples were assigned that duty. Yet one of their qualifications was that they were "full of the Spirit," which was therefore not a gift conferred on them by the apostolic laying on of hands. The apostles did not "delegate" any of their own functions to the seven, such as "the ministry," or "service," of preaching the word.

The Greek term *diakonos,* sometimes represented by "deacon" in the New Testament, was still used in the nontechnical sense of "servant" in Paul's letters. In this sense Paul applied it to himself as well as other apostles, to officers of the Roman government, and to Phoebe, a Christian woman from Cenchreae near Corinth. (I Corinthians 3:5; II Corinthians 3:6, 6:4, 11:23; Romans 13:4 and 16:1)

Probably, at some time early enough for the Christian church still to have acted under the influence of Jewish synagogue practices, the congregation at Jerusalem elected a council of "elders." Like the Jewish elders, they managed the financial affairs of the community, for it was to them that Paul and Barnabas delivered the relief collected and sent to the brethren in Judea by the disciples in Antioch. (Acts 11:27-30) Later these elders at Jerusalem met with the apostles there to decide matters of policy governing relations between Jewish and Gentile believers. (Acts 15:6-23) The only New Testament writer to use the Greek term *synagoge* for a Christian assembly also mentioned elders of the congregation or *ekklesia*. (James 2:2; 5:14) Although this letter was attributed to James the brother of Jesus, most scholars today believe it could not have been written much before A.D. 100.

It is uncertain how soon Christian churches outside Palestine adopted the institution of elders, but it must have been after Paul's death. Although he listed many other types of service in the church, Paul never mentioned elders in any genuine letter of his. Luke was unconsciously in error when he reported that Paul and Barnabas appointed elders in every church which they had established in the province of Galatia. (Acts 14:23) He repeated this mistake when he described Paul as summoning the elders of the church at Ephesus to meet him at Miletus. (Acts 20:17)

The chief value of this story lies in the light it sheds on the stage reached in the organization of the church when Luke wrote near the end of the first century. By that time Christian elders had acquired further duties. They were given these instructions: "Take heed to yourselves and to all the flock, in which the Holy Spirit has made you guardians, to feed the church of the Lord which he obtained with his own blood." (Acts 20:28) The word here translated "guardians" in modern English versions was represented by other words in earlier translations. The King James version had "overseers," but in the nineteenth century this was revised to read "bishops." Luke's Greek term was *episkopoi*, which was just the right word to describe shepherds whose duty it was to look after a flock. In this sense one writer applied the term *episkopos* to Christ himself: "For you were straying like sheep, but have now returned to the Shepherd and Guardian of your souls." (I Peter 2:25) Here the King James version said "bishop."

Whoever wrote this epistle attributed to Peter closed it with an exhortation to Christian elders, in which he described himself as a fellow elder and urged them to feed God's flock. In other words, elders were the same as the "pastors" mentioned in Ephesians 4:11. The writer went on to urge younger members of the congregation to be subject to the elders. Thus the term was still used as it had been in Judaism for the older men of the community whose chief claim to authority lay in their maturity and longer experience. (I Peter 5:1-5)

Although Paul never spoke of elders, he began one of his letters with greetings "to all the saints in Christ Jesus who are at Philippi, with the bishops and deacons." (Philippians 1:1) At least that is the usual translation. But we have already seen that in other letters Paul often used the Greek term *diakonos*, in the general sense of servant. So it is probable that he used the other term *episkopos* in a similar way. His letter to the Philippians was written to thank the congregation for some gift which they had sent to him in prison. This suggests that the "overseers" and "servants" whom he mentioned here were men in charge of the charitable funds from which that gift was drawn. (Philippians 4:10-18)

Whatever the duties of these "bishops" or "overseers" or "guardians" at Philippi, they acted as a committee or group. There is no evidence here or in any letter of Paul's to indicate a single presiding officer who served as chairman at meetings of the congregation. Had there been such a "president of the brethren" at Corinth, the disturbances which marred the gatherings for worship and the Lord's supper could never have happened. Even so, Paul did not try to solve the problem by directing the church to elect a "bishop" or by appointing one himself.

Steps like these were taken later by someone writing, in Paul's name, in the pastoral epistles. As we have seen, these three books were written to combat false doctrine. If that doctrine was the teaching of the Docetists, the date of the pastorals may have been as early as A.D. 100-110. But if it was Marcion's heresy, it would be about 140-150. Since Marcion recognized Paul as the only true apostle and claimed to teach what Paul had taught, it was natural for the church to oppose him in the name of Paul. So these epistles were addressed to Timothy and Titus, whose names were often mentioned in genuine letters of Paul as his younger assistants.

The Epistle to Titus took up the subject of the ministry at its very beginning:

> This is why I left you in Crete, that you might amend what was defective, and appoint elders in every town as I directed you, men who are blameless, married only once, whose children are believers and not open to the charge of being profligate or insubordinate. (Titus 1:5-6)

In other words, the writer felt something was still needed to complete the church's organization, and that was a council of elders in each community. However, the author went on immediately to list the qualifications required for a bishop, in fact according to the Greek text "the bishop," as if there were now to be only one in any particular place. The most likely conclusion from all this would be that one member of the council of elders was to be chosen or appointed to preside over their meetings, and perhaps also at meetings of the whole congregation. This is supported by the reference to "elders who rule" (or preside) in I Timothy 5:17.

Evidently one of the functions of the bishop was still to supervise the distribution of funds for charitable purposes, for he must not be "greedy for gain," nor a "lover of money." On the contrary, he should be "hospitable" in welcoming visiting members from other congregations. In addition to this, he must be able "to give instruction in sound doctrine and also to confute those who contradict it." Thus he was to combat heresy by teaching true doctrine. (Titus 1:7-9; I Timothy 3:2-7) The best method of doing this would be to transmit Christian tradition as it had been received from such apostles as Paul himself: "What you have heard from me before many witnesses entrust to faithful men who will be able to teach others also." (II Timothy 2:2)

By the end of the second century this had become one of the chief responsibilities of the bishops and the elders or *presbyteroi*, to use the Greek term. So Irenaeus said that apostolic tradition was preserved by the successions of presbyters in the churches. In refuting the Gnostics and other heretics, he claimed that it was possible to reckon up those who had been instituted as bishops by the apostles, and to trace the succession of such men to his own time. Irenaeus was particularly interested in drawing up a list of the bishops in the church at Rome, where Marcion had done his mischief. The apostles Peter and Paul, he said, entrusted the episcopate there to Linus, referring to II Timothy 4:21. He was succeeded by Anancletus, and Clement was allotted the bishopric in third place from the apostles. But another writer, named Tertullian, around A.D. 200, believed that Clement had been ordained by Peter, and he knew of no other bishop of Rome before Clement. Thus it is clear that by the end of the second century nobody had any very reliable information on the subject.

The pastoral epistles, even if they were genuine letters of an apostle, would lend no support to later theories of "apostolic succession." In the first place, there is real confusion in the letters about who actually "ordained" Timothy. In one of them the writer said: "I remind you to rekindle the gift of God that is within you through the laying on of my hands," as if ordination were a function performed by an apostle acting alone. (II Timothy 1:6) Yet in another letter, he gave an entirely different view of the matter: "Do not neglect the gift which you have, which was given you by prophetic utterance when the elders laid their hands upon you." (I Timothy 4:14) Here the ordination was by the whole presbytery, or council of elders, with no mention of an apostle at all.

Besides this confusion, there is the problem about what position in the church either Timothy or Titus was supposed to occupy. Timothy was pictured as having authority to ordain others, for he was warned not to be hasty in the laying on of hands. (I Timothy 5:22) Titus also had instructions to appoint elders, and was told the qualifications of a bishop, as well as of deacons. Yet neither of these two men were spoken of as being themselves either apostles, or bishops, or even elders. On the contrary, Timothy was urged to do the work of an evangelist. (II Timothy 4:5) That would seem to mean that an evangelist had full authority to ordain others by the laying on of hands. Whether a bishop had such authority is a matter about which the author of the pastorals was silent. Nor did he give any instructions about the possible duties of the bishop and elders in the conduct of public worship or in the administration of the sacraments. Such instructions must be sought outside the writings of the New Testament.

Beyond this stage in the development of the church's ministry the New Testament furnishes no information, and our story might seem to end here. Yet there exist other Christian writings which are at least as old as the pastoral epistles and several other late books of the Bible. Although these writings were highly valued by later generations of Christians, they were not included among the holy scriptures, chiefly because it was known that they were not the work of any of the apostles.

The earliest of these non-biblical Christian writings was called the First Epistle of Clement. Those who gave it this title had reason to believe it was written by Clement, whom Irenaeus listed as the third bishop of the Roman church, probably about A.D. 95. The letter was sent, by whoever was the actual author, in the name of the congregation in Rome to the congregation in Corinth. The Corinthian Christians were again divided into rival factions, as they had been in Paul's day, and had revolted against their presbyters. Those who had begun this revolt were therefore urged to repent and to be subject to the elders.

These elders were also called bishops or overseers, for the writer of the letter pronounced it no small sin to reject those who had blamelessly and devoutly offered the gifts of the episcopate. In his opinion this was an office to which men were appointed for life and which was of apostolic origin. He claimed that as the apostles had preached the gospel from place to place, they had appointed their first converts, after testing them by the Spirit, to be overseers and servants of those who would believe. In fact, the apostles had followed this procedure because they knew that there would be debate over the title of the episcopate. Since this letter always speaks of bishops or overseers in the plural, it seems to represent a period earlier than the pastoral epistles, where mention of "the bishop" in the singular suggests a single presiding officer.

It was Ignatius of Antioch (c. 112 A.D.), in his letters combatting the heresy of the Docetists, who first defended a hierarchy of three orders of ministers. In this system of church government, a single bishop presided over the presbytery or council of elders, assisted by deacons. Writing to the church at Smyrna, Ignatius insisted that no one should do anything pertaining to the church without the bishop. This rule applied to the administration of baptism and the Lord's supper, which Ignatius referred to as a Eucharist or Thanksgiving. Such a service should be regarded as valid only if performed by the bishop, or by someone to whom he had entrusted it. Ignatius went on to say: "Wherever the bishop appears, there let the people be, just as wherever Jesus Christ is present, there is the universal church." This was apparently the first time in history that the term "catholic" was applied to the whole body of believers throughout the world.

To other Asiatic churches, Ignatius repeated his exhortation: "Do nothing without the bishop." But in his letter to the church at Rome he made no mention of the episcopate, except to refer to himself as the bishop of Syria. He was able to mention the bishop of several churches by name, but he evidently knew of no individual whom he might address as bishop of Rome. Later, Hermas, the Roman author of *The Shepherd*, in using the term "bishop" always did so in the plural, never the singular. However, he stated that after he had written his book he was commissioned to read it publicly "with the elders who preside over the church."

It is generally recognized that the Greek term *presbyteros*, meaning "elder," has given us not only the English word "presbyter," but also by contraction the word "priest." Nevertheless, in both the Old and New Testaments, priests were always clearly distinguished from elders, both in name and in function. The Greek term for "priest" is *hiereus*, from which we derive the term "hierarchy." It means a "holy" person, one consecrated and set apart for the worship and service of God. In Judaism, as in other ancient religions, the chief function of the priests was the offering of sacrifices. The elders performed an entirely different function in the community. Like Roman "senators," they were elected for their maturity and wisdom to govern the people. They had no connection whatever with the service of the temple and the altar. The fact that certain councils among the Jews were said to have been composed of both "chief priests and elders of the people" indicates plainly that the two terms were in no way synonymous. (Matthew 27:1; Acts 4:23; 23:14)

Thus when the Christian community adopted from Judaism the institution of presbyters or elders, this did not mean the establishment of an order of priesthood. The religious outlook of the earliest Christians made such an institution unnecessary. For they were convinced that, through Christ, God had established a new covenant with his people. Consequently, the old covenant was obsolete, and the sacrifices offered under that covenant were abolished. (Hebrews 8:6-13; 10:1-18) The priests of the old covenant had had to stand daily at their service, offering repeatedly the same sacrifices which could never take away sins. But Christ had come to do the will of God, and in so doing had offered for all time a single sacrifice for sins, which need not and cannot be repeated, since it consisted of the offering of himself. (Hebrews 9:24-26; 10:5-10) For those who thought of the work of Christ in these terms, his life was the fulfillment of a divine promise made in scripture: "You are a priest forever after the order of Melchizedek." (Psalm 110:4; Hebrews 5:6)

The First Epistle of Clement likewise reflects this conception of Christ as "high priest." Writing to the church at Philadelphia, Ignatius of Antioch also made a rather obscure reference to the central theme of Hebrews: "The priests [he wrote] were good, but better is the high priest who has been entrusted with the holy of holies, who alone has been entrusted with the secrets of God." It is obvious that this "high priest" is Christ himself. And since the favorite word of the writer of Hebrews is "better," as he stresses the superiority of Christ and his covenant to the old, the other "priests" mentioned by Ignatius must be those of the Levitical line of the Old Testament.

Although the Old Testament had established a special order of priests appointed from the tribe of Levi, God had commanded Moses to say to all the people of Israel: "You shall be to me a kingdom of priests and a holy nation." (Exodus 19:6) New Testament writers held that this text of scripture too had been fulfilled, for they applied it to the whole community of believers. (I Peter 2:5, 9; Revelation 1:6; 5:10) This doctrine that all believers are "priests to God" has profound significance for the life of the church, wherever and whenever it is taken seriously. For it means that every Christian has the vocation to be a "minister," or servant, of God.

Since the word *hiereus* or "priest" means quite literally a person who is "holy," it coincides exactly with the frequently repeated reminder that all members of the church are "called to be saints." (Romans 1:7; I Corinthians 1:2; Ephesians 1:1; Philippians 1:1; Colossians 1:2) Both words describe a person whose life is "sanctified" or, in other words, dedicated to the service of God. The New Testament speaks of God himself as consecrating believers completely. (I Thessalonians 5:23) It also declares that such consecration is accomplished in Christ, or in his name, and by the Holy Spirit. (I Corinthians 1:2; 6:11; Romans 15:16)

Like every true priest, a saint is first of all a person who worships God. Under the old covenant worship had always included the sacrifice of animal victims, but under the new covenant all that came to an end forever. In order to accomplish the will of God, Jesus Christ had offered his body once for all to the endurance of suffering and death. It is by that offering that believers have been consecrated. (Hebrews 10:8-10; 14) This means that they are to share Christ's life of self-offering to God. They are called to present their bodies as a "living sacrifice," holy and acceptable to him. (Romans 12:1-2) In calling this "your reasonable service," the English version of 1611 was really more accurate than the latest revision, which says, "your spiritual worship." Paul's Greek adjective *logikos,* from which we get our word "logical," implies that the primitive practice of presenting to God the slain bodies of dumb beasts was an irrational form of worship. Worship which is truly acceptable to God involves the consecration of all that we are—body, mind, and every other faculty—to God's will. It likewise includes the consecration of all that we possess, for it means "to do good and to share what you have." (Hebrews 13:15-16) These great insights of the New Testament are of the utmost importance for Christian worship, as well as for our understanding of the church as the community of people dedicated to the service of God, the Father of our Lord Jesus Christ.

CONCLUSION

No ONE who follows in the New Testament the story of the church from its beginnings in the mission of Jesus Christ to the congregation of Israel can fail to be impressed with the amazing transformation produced by the gospel under the powerful leading of the Holy Spirit. At the heart of everything in those records, there is what Paul called "a new creation" in Christ. "The old has passed away, behold, the new has come." (II Corinthians 5:17) Such a transformation, as Paul urged, must always begin with a renewal of the "mind" of the believer. (Romans 12:2) The apostle was confident that Christians "have the mind of Christ." (I Corinthians 2:16) They are called to share the same mutual love for one another, the same willingness to subordinate self-interest to the interests of others, the same humility of mind and the same sacrificial obedience to God which characterized the thinking of Christ himself. (Philippians 2:1-8) It is to such a "change of mind" that the gospel summons men when it says: "Repent, for the kingdom of heaven is at hand." (Matthew 3:1; 4:17)

The men who wrote the books that make up the New Testament believed that they were living in "the last days." They were eagerly looking for "the age to come." The idea that the coming of the Messiah would inaugurate a new creation was part of their eschatology. Near the end of the last book in the New Testament, the writer described a prophetic vision of a new heaven and a new earth. And he who sat on the throne said, "Behold,

I make all things new." (Revelation 21:1, 5) After nineteen centuries of continuing history, during which the church has pursued its mission to the world, that vision and that promise are far from being realized. Nevertheless, the conviction that the living God does create the new to replace the old is one penetrating insight in the ultimate hopes of those earliest Christians which retains permanent validity. For those who first voiced that hope discovered from personal experience, what the church has to learn again and again, that the coming of Jesus Christ into this world not only demanded, but actually effected, sweeping changes in their own lives.

All the original disciples of the Lord Jesus were brought up, as he himself had been, in the age-old traditions of the Hebrew scriptures, nurtured and centered in synagogue and temple. For them, membership in the church came as no new discovery, for it was a long-accepted fact. Yet this very basic fact had to be thoroughly rethought in the light of their recognition of the Messiah in the person of the crucified. One of the most ardent apostles of the gospel of Christ crucified had at first resisted it to the point of violent persecution. The beginning of the new creation in Paul's life may have been determined by one decisive moment, such as the Acts describe in the vision on the Damascus road. Yet Paul's own letters suggest that the most profound and far-reaching changes in his old ways of thinking about God's dealing with men were the result of a long and painful process of growth. In fact, his most distinctive Christian convictions were reached, through agonizing searchings of heart, during the course of an intense controversy with his more conservative brethren of Jewish descent. It was this struggle to secure the inclusion of Gentile converts within the Christian fellowship, on terms of complete equality with Jewish believers, that gave to the church—in the providence of God—its truly universal character. The New Testament simply affirms this unity of all believers to be a fact: "There is neither Jew nor Greek, there is neither slave nor free, there is neither male nor female; for you are all one in Christ Jesus." (Galatians 3:28) Yet it was this fact which demanded the most drastic revision of men's habitual ways of thinking and living. That is as true today as it was at the beginning.

If the lordship of Jesus required radical alterations in the thought and conduct of Jewish believers, the new habits which it exacted of pagan converts was nothing short of revolutionary. For men and women steeped for generations in pagan beliefs and practices, conversion to Christ meant far more than a re-interpretation of long-cherished ideas and expectations or even their fulfillment in fresh ways. Most Gentile converts had more to "unlearn" than did Jewish believers. Their new faith in God, the Father of the Lord Jesus Christ, called for the repudiation of their former polytheism and idolatry, of gross superstition and immorality. At the same time, the gift of the Holy Spirit incor-porated them into a community united by ties of brotherhood such as they had never before known. There was nothing in the former experience of converts from paganism which corre-sponded even remotely to this fact of membership in the church, and very little to prepare them for it.

It is true, of course, that Stoic moralists, as well as other phi-losophers of the time, condemned antisocial vices and extolled virtues which tended toward unselfishness and cooperation. Yet there is little reason to suppose that such philosophical ethics had any marked influence on the masses of Gentile people to whom the gospel had to be preached. Some of the most popu-lar religious cults of the Hellenistic age were those known as the "mysteries." These cults won their adherents by a promise of in-dividual immortality, as well as present escape from cruel fate, through secret rites which were claimed to bring about union with the deity. But there is nothing to indicate that entrance into the mysteries ever gave to initiates a vivid sense of belong-ing to "one body," in which they became "members one of another." In such religions "salvation" was always a private affair, and moral standards were seldom high. How different was the gospel message of redemption. Faith in God, the Father of the Lord Jesus Christ, carried with it, as twin corollaries, the assurance of being "children of God" and the obligation of living together in mutual love of the brethren.

The transforming power of Christ affected everything that he touched. It altered the very meaning of the words which believers used to describe who he is and what he has done. The fresh light that radiates from the old terms is indicative of a transfiguration wrought in the fundamental realities to which they were intended to refer. Most of the key words in the vocabulary of the New Testament were drawn more or less directly from the language of the Old. We have observed how frequently such characteristically biblical terms acquired hitherto unsuspected significance to the earliest Christians: "covenant," "church," "holy," "Messiah," "priest," "sacrifice," to name but a few. The same thing is especially true of more common words like "faith," "fellowship," "love," which are so often only vaguely understood, when they are not actually misused.

Yet the first thing that a reader of the New Testament needs to acquire is not necessarily a new dictionary, although there are Bible wordbooks which can be of real help to him. Probably the primary requirement of anyone who seeks to understand the teaching of the New Testament—and the writer confesses his own constant need of this—is what Paul called "the renewal of your mind." This surely implies a willingness to be led by the Spirit, accepting, where necessary, some revision of our preconceived notions about the meaning of any particular text of scripture. If we believe that the living God continues his revealing work among believers, it implies readiness to "hear what the Spirit says to the churches," by pondering prayerfully each passage that we read. It is only through such devotional reading that the Bible can speak to our hearts as the word of God. Central to every true understanding of the scriptures is Christ, the Word made flesh.

Since the New Testament testifies that Christianity has from the first been a corporate, never a purely private, affair, the revival of the practice of group study of the Bible is one of the most promising signs of our times. We have much to learn from one another as we share the deepest concerns of our common life in Christ. While it is to be expected that Bible study groups will usually be formed of members of the same local congregation, and consequently of the same communion, more inclusive circles are urgently needed. All who profess and call themselves Christians constantly need to enlarge their knowledge of the faith which they confess, by searching the scriptures which bear witness to Christ. Yet differing ways of interpreting the Bible, conflicting understandings even of the same text, have helped to create and perpetuate the unhappy divisions which hinder the church's mission to the world. These divisions are not likely to be healed, unless members of each branch of the church universal are prepared to make sincere and sympathetic efforts to understand the biblical basis of doctrines and practices which characterize other Christian communions as well as their own. Through shared study and discussion of the meaning of the gospel, undertaken in humble devotion to the one Lord, we may yet come to a fuller realization of the fundamental convictions which unite us in his service.

It is to the books of the New Testament, especially, that all Christians must constantly look as they take council together for the future. In these books the church can be seen taking its first steps upon a long road beset with dangerous pitfalls. Threatened with pagan superstitions and false doctrines, the church was supported by the Old Testament to maintain in its creeds the prophetic faith of Israel in one God, Creator of heaven and earth. Against each new attack of heresy, it reaffirmed the apostolic proclamation that Jesus Christ is God's unique Son, our Lord, who died and rose again for us according to the scriptures. Assured that, in him, God had made a new covenant with his people, sealed by the gift of his Holy Spirit, the church received the writings of Paul and other apostolic men as further revelations of the mind of Christ. Deeply conscious of its own unity and consecration, created by the presence of the Spirit, the church affirmed the communion of saints, the forgiveness of sins, through Christ, and the hope of resurrection to eternal life.

Through the pages of the New Testament, we can also trace some of the earliest attempts of the church to order its corporate life. The apostles, commissioned by the risen Lord, spoke with the personal authority of eyewitnesses. Other men, endowed by the Holy Spirit with special gifts as prophets and teachers, were also recognized as speaking with the authority of divine inspiration. Pastors and evangelists, healers and workers of miracles, also exercised special ministries. In the congregation in Jerusalem, at least, elders took part in the councils of the apostles. Later, as the number of local congregations multiplied, it became necessary to provide for the administration of the charitable relief of the poor, an obligation which was closely associated with the celebration of the Lord's supper. Eventually the supervision of these services was to be entrusted to the bishops, assisted by the deacons. At the beginning of the second century, writings outside the New Testament collection indicate that the office of bishop was beginning to be distinguished from that of the elders or presbyters. Before the end of that century, defenders of the true faith against false doctrines could point to a succession of tradition from one bishop to the next as a guarantee of apostolic authority. Summaries of this apostolic faith formed the nucleus of the creeds. But at the basis of those creeds lay the New Testament itself. Together the scriptures of the Old and New Testaments still constitute the essential groundwork for determining true Christian doctrine. On this there is general agreement.

Richardson, Cyril C. *The Church Through the Centuries.* New York: Charles Scribner's Sons, 1938.

Robinson, William. *The Biblical Doctrine of the Church.* St. Louis: The Bethany Press, 1948.

Scott, Ernest F. *The Nature of the Early Church.* New York: Charles Scribner's Sons, 1941.

Wand, J. W. C. *The Church: Its Nature, Structure, and Function.* New York: Morehouse-Gorham Company, 1948.

Wedel, Theodore O. *The Coming Great Church.* New York: The Macmillan Company, 1945.

INDEX TO SCRIP-
TURAL PASSAGES

GENERAL INDEX

185